A PETERHEAD PORTRAIT

Jim Buchan

The Buchan Field Club
Occasional Publication No. 2

Produced in association with

Aberdeenshire
COUNCIL

Peterhead 1997

Aberdeenshire Heritage photographs from the Arbuthnot Museum, Peterhead are reproduced by permission of Aberdeenshire Council, Leisure & Recreation Department.

ISBN 0 9512736 2 0

Published by the Buchan Field Club

Printed and bound by BPC-AUP Aberdeen Ltd.

EDITOR'S PREFACE

Jim Buchan was born in Inverallochy. He was educated at the village school and at Fraserburgh Academy before going to the University of Aberdeen, where he graduated M.A. (Hons.) in History in 1949 and M.Ed. in 1954. He taught in schools in Aberdeenshire and the City of Aberdeen for 23 years and then was Rector of Peterhead Academy for 16 years, before retiring in 1991. Jim Buchan was President of the Buchan Field Club for 11 years and retired from this office in 1996. A Fellow of the Society of Antiquaries of Scotland (F.S.A.Scot.), he is the author of *A School History of Aberdeenshire* (1961), *Bygone Buchan* (1987), *Peterhead in Old Picture Postcards* (1992), and *Peterhead and District in Old Picture Postcards* (1995). This latest book represents the results of his research over the past few years into the extensive collection of photographs of old Peterhead held at the Arbuthnot Museum.

David M. Bertie

PREFACE AND ACKNOWLEDGEMENTS

My thanks are due to many people -- too numerous to name individually here -- without whose help the production of *A Peterhead Portrait* would not have been possible. Over the years, I had become interested in the Victorian items in the photographic collection in the Arbuthnot Museum, Peterhead. With the "spare time" available after retiring, but with no intention of publishing any results, I began to "research" this archive. The co-operation of the members of the staff of the North East of Scotland Museums Service -- in particular the Museums Curator, Ms Jocelyn Chamberlain-Mole; the Depute Curator, Dr. David Bertie; and the Photographer, Rex Findlay -- was of paramount importance in this. After the re-organisation of local government and the establishment of Aberdeenshire Heritage in April 1996, this co-operation continued; for that, my thanks are due to Andrew Hill, Principal Curator, and Richard Findlay, Leisure & Recreation Administrative Officer.

Members of the staff in Peterhead Public Library have been most helpful as have the staff in the headquarters of the North East of Scotland Library Service (now Aberdeenshire Library & Information Service) in Oldmeldrum.

When my research extended furth of Peterhead, I was given valuable assistance by the staff in the University of Aberdeen's Special Collections and Archives; James Dun's House, Aberdeen Art Gallery & Museums; West Register House and the National Library of Scotland, Edinburgh; the Mitchell Library, Glasgow; the National Museum of Photography, Film, and Television, Bradford; and The Royal Photographic Society, Bath. Help was also forthcoming during correspondence with Roderick McDonald, Rider University, New Jersey; and with staff in libraries and museums in Washington and Philadelphia, U.S.A.; Sydney and Melbourne, Australia; and Dunedin, New Zealand.

Professor Derek Holton, University of Otago, New Zealand, was instrumental in initiating a most fruitful correspondence involving Ian Church of the Port Chalmers Museum; Ian Farquhar, Dunedin; Wayne Matheson, Southland, New Zealand (great-grandson of Peterheadian, James Matheson of the *Yarra*!); Ronald Parsons of the Australian Maritime Historical Society; and William Volum (descendant of Captain James Volum, the Peterhead whaler!), the secretary of the Nautical Association of Australia.

I am extremely grateful to Angus and Valerie McDonald for their invaluable assistance during the preparation of the camera-ready copy for the printers; in this connection, thanks are also due to Pat Penrose and Alen McKenzie.

Dr. David Bertie, as Hon. Editor of Publications for the Buchan Field Club, suggested that I should publish an account of my researches. He, therefore, deserves some credit for any merit which *A Peterhead Portrait* may have. I am solely responsible for all errors of omission and commission.

Jim Buchan, February 1997

CONTENTS

1   Introductory: The *Art-Science*

8   "Practisers of the Popular Art"

15   William L. Taylor: *Peterhead and its Environs in Stereoscope*

26   Joseph Collier: *The Howes o' Buchan*

35   James Shivas: *Photographic Artist*

45   Peterhead Free Library and Arbuthnot Museum

55   "Our Greenland Fleet"

69   "Saut Herrin"

80   Peterhead-built

107   The Volunteer Movement

ILLUSTRATIONS

I wish to express my thanks to those who have given permission for the reproduction of photographs for which they hold the copyright.

Each illustration has been assigned a letter according to the chapter in which it is featured: for example, all the illustrations in the first chapter may be identified by the letter *A*, while *D* is the distinguishing letter for those in the fourth chapter. In addition, the illustrations in each chapter have been numbered serially and so the fourth photograph in the third chapter will be *C4*, while the fourth illustration in the sixth chapter will be *F4*.

Illustrations *A1*, *A3*, *A6*, and *A7* have been reproduced courtesy of the National Museums of Scotland.

Illustrations *A2*, *A4*, and the photograph of a Victorian camera which appears on the cover have been used courtesy of the Aberdeen Camera Club.

Illustration *C5* appears courtesy of the University of Aberdeen.

Private individuals have granted permission for the use of the following specimens from their albums:- *B2*, *C6*, *D2*, *D3*, *D4*, *D5*, *D6*, *D7*, *E3*, *E8*, *E9*, *E17*, *E18*, *E19*, *E20*, *E21*, and *K3*.

Illustrations *D17*, *D18*, *D19*, *D20*, and *D21* are published courtesy of Malcolm E. Collier, a great-grandson of Joseph Collier.

Wayne J. Matheson, a great-grandson of Captain James Matheson of the *Yarra*, supplied illustration *J10*.

The Joseph Collier photographs, *D8*, *D9*, *D10*, *D11*, *D12*, *D13*, *D14*, *D15*, and *D16*, have been reproduced by Aberdeenshire Heritage from *The Howes o' Buchan*, a copy of which was supplied by Aberdeenshire Library and Information Service.

None of the illustrations listed above is in the Arbuthnot Museum collections.

Copies of all the other illustrations may be purchased from the Arbuthnot Museum by contacting the Curator of Local History, Aberdeenshire Heritage, Aden Country Park, Mintlaw, Peterhead, Aberdeenshire AB42 5FQ.

INTRODUCTORY : The *Art-Science*

The invention of photography - the first practicable versions of which were the daguerreotype and the calotype - was one of the scientific wonders of the Victorian world.

Louis-Jacques Daguerre's invention of the daguerreotype was announced to the French House of Deputies on 7th January, 1839, and a description of the process was published in August that year. Only one image, permanently fixed on highly polished silver or silvered copper, could be obtained as a result of each operation, which was carried out using a range of costly equipment. Long exposure times, requiring the total immobility of the subject, were necessary and success depended on a process which involved lengthy and precise chemical manipulations, some of them carried out in a room which was completely lightproof.

Shortly before details of his methods were published in France, Daguerre patented the process in England.

The patent rights did not apply to Scotland but the high cost of the equipment and materials used, as well as the not inconsiderable chemical knowledge and technical skill required, meant that there was no immediate rush by natives of the north-east neuk to join the ranks of the professional daguerreotypists.

Aberdeen's first professional portrait photographers, itinerant daguerreotypists Watson and Fannin, opened their "Gallery" at 69, Union Street on 25th July, 1842. After visiting the studio, a reporter for *The Aberdeen Herald* came close to pronouncing the daguerreotype process to be the eighth wonder of the world. "The production of portraits so accurate and beautiful by means apparently so simple," he wrote, "like the illusions of the magic lantern, or the more useful applications of steam and gas, has a tendency to carry one back to the age of miracles, or rather to raise a doubt whether the marvellous feats attributed in eastern tales and northern legends to genii, fairies, and other unearthly beings, may not soon be excelled

A1 A daguerreotypist's paraphernalia, including a Gaudin-type camera made in Paris in 1841.

1

by the genius, skill, and perseverance of mortal man." He told his readers that, paradoxically, although the quality of the natural light was the most important factor "in this wonderful process of portrait painting - or rather portrait engraving", some of the best portraits had been taken on days which were looked upon as dull. Emphasising that a daguerreotypist required a working knowledge of the chemicals used and had to be "a steady manipulator" who exercised the greatest care in every stage of the process, he surely left his readers more mystified than ever by his synoptic description of the process. "To bring out the picture," he said, "there must be a heating, a cooling, a wetting, a drying, a wiping, a blowing - a hanging over mercury and under spring water - a hot bath, and a blast from the mouth. These operations are gone through partly in a dark chamber, amid fumes that would turn the nose of any delicate belle who should venture to follow her portrait in its journey from seeming nothing to life-like light and shadow, and partly in a laboratory amid spirit lamps and other chemical and mechanical apparatus."

be closed for a short period while they visited Inverness. When they re-opened their gallery on 1st December, they informed potential customers that their stay in Aberdeen would, "from arrangements they had entered into in the north, be necessarily short." Before the end of the month, they reiterated that their stay in Aberdeen would be limited and announced that they had "resolved, in order to meet the wishes of many inquirers, to make a considerable Reduction in their Charges." A single portrait would be taken for 10s.6d. (52½p) and a suitable case or frame supplied for 5s. (25p). Even then, only the well-to-do could afford to have a daguerreotype taken.

For several years thereafter, daguerreotypists were active in north-eastern Scotland. For example, in May, 1849, J. Henderson established a studio in Banff; in April, 1850, Alex. Rae, a chemist in Banff, announced that he would be taking daguerreotypes; and, as late as 1862, John Nisbet was still practising the art in Market Street, Aberdeen, but the technique never attained widespread popularity in the area and,

A2 A daguerreotype with a case; daguerreotypist unidentified; date unknown.

Daguerreotypes, costing £1.1s (£1.05) for a "Single Miniature in a neat Case or Frame", were far beyond the reach of most Aberdonians and so it was not merely snobbishness which led the pioneer photographers to address their original advertisement to "the Nobility and Gentry of Aberdeen and its vicinity". Presumably they did not patronise the newfangled studio in sufficient numbers to keep the daguerreotypists steadily occupied for, within ten weeks of their opening in Aberdeen, Watson and Fannin intimated that their Operating Rooms would

as far as is known, no daguerreotypes were produced in Peterhead.

Spurred on by reports from Paris that Louis Daguerre had invented a "photographic" process, William Fox Talbot, who had been investigating the use of light-sensitive chemicals since the mid-1830s, showed specimens of his "photogenic drawings" to members of the Royal Society in London on 31st January, 1839. He continued his experiments and, in 1841, patented a much-improved process in which exposure times were reduced to a matter of minutes. This was the *calotype* process which, in later years, was aptly known as the *paper negative/positive* process. It was cheaper and easier to use than the daguerreotype process but it was still essential for the calotypist to be skilled in the appropriate chemical manipulations necessary for the production, on specially sensitised paper, of a developed image. The exact reverse of the original image, this was called the "negative" and an unlimited number of "positive" prints could be made from it. As a result, the commercial development of photography became a more feasible proposition. Portrait photographers could supply multiple copies at reduced rates and it was much easier to take photographs in the open air. In the mid-1840s, for example, Fox Talbot produced his series of pictures associated with the works of Sir Walter Scott, *Sun Pictures in Scotland,* and also the first photographically illustrated book, *The Pencil of Nature.*

A3 A calotype camera made about 1840.

Sir David Brewster, Principal of the United Colleges of St. Leonard and St. Salvator in St. Andrews and famous for his experiments on the diffraction of light, played an important role in the development of photography in Scotland. Having learned about the calotype process through his correspondence with Fox Talbot, he helped Dr. John Adamson, a surgeon and erstwhile teacher of Chemistry in Madras College, St. Andrews, who had been experimenting with photography, to become the first to produce a calotype print in Scotland. John Adamson taught the art to his brother, Robert, who set up a studio in Edinburgh in May, 1843. Within two months, he formed a partnership with David Octavius Hill, a landscape and genre painter, to whom he had been introduced by Sir David Brewster. In the next three years, Hill and Adamson took about 3000 calotypes and published several volumes of their photographs.

The calotype process was adopted more widely than the daguerreotype but, although improvements were made to both, photography remained the preserve of a very small number of practitioners until Frederick Scott Archer, a sculptor and calotype photographer, announced details of a new photographic technique, the *collodion wet plate.* A clean glass plate was coated with collodion, which was formed by dissolving gun cotton in ether or alcohol mixed with potassium iodide. The plate was then sensitized by a coating of silver nitrate. It had to be exposed while still wet, then developed and fixed immediately after exposure. Although preparation of the plate was a messy business and, in some ways, the wet collodion process was more difficult to use than the daguerreotype or calotype, it produced a better image, reduced exposure times to a matter of seconds, and gave multiple copies from one negative. Archer did not patent his process when he introduced it in March, 1851, and it was quickly adopted by pioneer photographers.

The first collodion photograph produced in Aberdeenshire is said to have been taken in the Upper Kirkgate, Aberdeen, by George Duncan, optician to Aberdeen University. George Washington Wilson, an Aberdeen-based artist specialising in portrait miniatures, began taking collodion photographs professionally in 1852 and soon established himself as one of the leading exponents of the technique. In 1855, he published *A Practical Guide To The Collodion Process In Photography; Describing The Method Of Obtaining Collodion Negatives, And Of Printing From Them.* Within a few years, several photographers in the Peterhead area were using the process.

The obvious inconvenience in the wet collodion process, of having to prepare the plates immediately before exposure and develop them immediately afterwards, was eventually removed completely, in the 1870s, with the introduction of commercially produced dry plates.

The first practical step towards this was the result of experiments by Dr. Hill Norris who, in 1856, was granted a patent for his process of producing dry plates. He established a factory at Yardley, a suburb of Birmingham, where the plates were coated with a solution of gum arabic or gelatin, dried, and then packed in boxes for sale. Norris claimed that his dry collodion plates, which were being sold in Inverness, for example, in 1858, would "keep good for at least twelve months and may be developed days or weeks after exposure, producing excellent results".

Initially, the dry plate process required twice the exposure times of the wet collodion method. After Norris and others had carried out further experiments with the former, details of the first truly successful gelatin dry plate, which was produced by R. L. Maddox, were published in the *British Journal of Photography* on 8th September, 1871. In the next few years, further improvements were made in the dry plate process as a result of experiments by, among others, Richard Kennett and Charles Bennett, and commercially produced dry plates, with exposure times of less than a second, were being sold by at least three firms before the end of the decade.

In October, 1879, for example, an advertisement extolling the advantages of *SWAN'S DRY PLATES* appeared in the *British Journal of Photography*. "These plates," it announced, "being ten times more sensitive than plates prepared by the wet collodion process, give new power to the Photographer, enabling him to take Views, Portraits, etc. under conditions of light that would, with the wet collodion process, have been quite impracticable. They are perfectly adapted to the general work of the Photographic Studio. By means of these plates, portraits of children can be taken with ease and certainty in any well-lighted glass house and even in the ordinary rooms of dwelling houses, where windows are large, portraits may be obtained without undue protraction of the sitting. They are suitable for landscape views and for what are called instantaneous views, and they possess many advantages for copying pictures, for interiors, for map copying, and all the work of the Photographer; also for enlarging, for copying negatives, and making lantern transparencies. The cleanliness and simplicity of the manipulation connected with the use of the plates, coupled with the certainty and excellence of the result obtainable by their means, must bring them into favour with both amateur and professional photographer." Ten different sizes of plates were available and the suppliers, Mawson and Swan, Newcastle-on-Tyne, also sold "Special light-tight boxes for storing and carrying dry plates." Plates measuring 12 inches by 10 inches cost 26s.6d (£1.32½) per dozen and the appropriate box cost 15s.6d (77½p); and a dozen 5 by 4 inch plates cost 4s.3d (21½p), while the box cost 8s.6d (42½p).

Freed from the complex and inhibiting chemical processes of the earlier years, photography became increasingly a hobby for the well-to-do amateur, especially since a portable darkroom was no longer an essential item of equipment for outdoor work. This trend was accelerated after George Eastman of Rochester, U.S.A., patented the first *Kodak* camera in

1888. With the slogan, "You press the button, we do the rest", he promoted the "instrument which altogether removes from the practice of photography the necessity for exceptional facilities, or, in fact, any special knowledge. It can be employed without preliminary study or a darkroom and without chemicals." Professional photographers, however, in Peterhead as elsewhere, continued to use the dry plate camera which, by the end of the century, had exposure times as low as one fiftieth of a second.

A4 A late Victorian Perken tailboard camera.

While the Victorians heralded photography as one of the more remarkable scientific discoveries of their age, they also regarded it as an art and often called it an *art-science*. Photographers were *artists of the lens* whose prints - portraits or "likenesses" and landscapes or "views" - were subjected to artistic criticism similar to that applied to the works of traditional portrait and landscape painters. At the same time, many of the early practitioners described themselves as *Artists and Photographers*, *Photographic Artists*, or *Artistic Photographers*.

The burgeoning popularity of photography was encouraged by royal patronage. Queen Victoria bought her first daguerreotype in 1840; posed, with the Prince of Wales, for her first calotype portrait in the mid-1840s; and collected photographs until the end of her reign, by which time she had filled more than a hundred albums. She was impressed by the latest stereoscopes displayed at the Great Exhibition in 1851 and began to add stereoscopic photographs, or stereographs, to her collection.

A stereograph consists of two apparently identical pictures mounted side by side. The pictures are not identical but the difference between them is usually so insignificant as to be not readily detectable by the naked eye. When viewed through a stereoscope, the two "flat", two-dimensional pictures are combined into one "solid", three-dimensional picture, a transformation which, in the words of one Victorian journalist, "is one of the most pleasing as well as one of the most wonderful in the science of optics". Initially, the two pictures were taken individually, with an ordinary camera, from a slightly different viewpoint and then mounted together. One of the stereographs in the local collection, *A5 North Bridge, Edinburgh*, below, is an example of this. While the details are seemingly similar, there is a man on the pavement in the bottom right corner, in the left hand picture, who is not in the "matching" half!

In later years, a stereo camera (as shown below), with two lenses positioned side by side, was used to take the two pictures simultaneously.

The stereoscopes which had impressed Queen Victoria in 1851 were developed as a result of the researches of Sir David Brewster, the Scottish

A5 North Bridge, Edinburgh; the Calton Hill behind and Market Street in the foreground.

A6 Stereo camera made in London in 1862.

physicist who invented the kaleidoscope. He presented his ideas for a much-improved stereoscope, using lenses to combine the slightly dissimilar pictures of the stereograph, at a meeting of the British Association for the Advancement of Science in Birmingham in 1849. A few lenticular instruments were made in Scotland, mostly in Dundee, but failed to attract much attention. Brewster's invention was well received, however, at a meeting of the Imperial Institute of France which was held in Paris at the end of December, 1850. Some daguerreotype views were produced and, with a number of the new-style stereoscopes, were shown at the Great Exhibition.

"stereomania" - a nationwide interest in the acquisition of stereoscopes and stereographs. George Washington Wilson, for example, with his customary business acumen, was quick to take advantage of the situation. He issued his first list of stereoscopic views, mostly of scenes in and around Aberdeen and Deeside, and continued to produce stereographs of locations in Scotland and England for several years thereafter. Peterhead was not immune from the craze. By 1859, stereoscpoes and stereographs were on sale in the town and local photographers were prepaired to take stereoscopic photographs, landscapes as well as portraits.

A7 Lenticular stereoscope made about 1855.

Almost coincidentally with the introduction of the lenticular stereoscope, Scott Archer had published details of his collodion wet plate process and, by 1858, Hill Norris was advertising "Dry Collodion Plates for Stereoscopic Negatives". The collodion process led to the easier and cheaper production of glass transparencies and paper prints. The latter were more durable for everyday use and, as further improvements were made to the stereoscope to admit sufficient light for the paper prints to be viewed clearly, paper stereographs became universally popular.

The interaction of developments in photography with developments in optics, together with the seal of royal approval bestowed by Queen Victoria, triggered a

In 1854, a Frenchman named Andre Disderi patented the carte-de-visite - an albumen silver print pasted on to a card. Disderi published a *carte-de-visite* portrait of Napoleon III in 1859 and, in the following year, John Mayall produced the first series of royal cartes-de-visite in Britain. In the next two years, two more royal series were published. Once again, royal patronage fostered a mania. On this occasion, it was "cartomania", an enthusiasm for filling albums with cartes-de-visite of the family; for a while, cameras taking several portraits on one plate were used to help to keep pace with the demand. In common with photographers elsewhere, Peterhead's artists of the lens were not slow to cash in on the craze.

The examples of cartes-de-visite on page 7 - *A8*

GENERALS OF THE SOUTH.

OUR PRESENT PEACE COMMISSIONERS.

A8 Generals of the South.

A9 Our Present Peace Commissioners.

Generals of the South and **A9 Our Present Peace Commissioners** - are reproduced in actual size. The former shows the commanders of the Confederate army, including Stonewall Jackson and Robert E. Lee. Ulysses Grant; W. T. Sherman, who made the march through Georgia to the sea; and G. H. Thomas, who was known as "the rock of Chickmauga", are among the leaders of the Union army shown on the latter. How these far-travelled momentoes of the American Civil War in the 1860s came to be preserved in the collection in the Arbuthnot Museum is a mystery but their presence there is a graphic illustration of the universality of the cartomania.

Mathew Brady, who had opened a photographic studio in New York in 1844, realised the potential of the camera as "the eye of history". He and others, including Paisley-born Alex Gardner, who published a *Photographic Sketch Book of the War*, documented the American Civil War. The work of such pioneers - for example, Francis Frith, who trekked eight hundred miles in the 1850s to photograph scenes in the valley of the River Nile; Roger Fenton, who covered the Crimean War in his horse-drawn "photographic carriage"; and Thomas Annan, who

published *Old Closes and Streets of Glasgow,* a collection of photographs of buildings earmarked for demolition during a slum clearance programme in the city in 1868-71 - heralded the dawn of the age of documentary photography and photographic journalism.

On a less dramatic level, photographers such as James Valentine of Dundee and Aberdeen-based George Washington Wilson published "views" of buildings, streets, landscapes, and aspects of daily life and work. By so doing, they created a valuable archive of the social history of Victorian Scotland.

On a much smaller scale, artists of the lens, who were active in the Peterhead area, produced a similar archive - the Victorian photographs in the Arbuthnot Museum, Peterhead. Prints from this collection, and the contemporaneous comments in the local press and other publications regarding the photographers and their subjects, have furnished the material for *A PETERHEAD PORTRAIT,* which is not intended to be a history of the town in the second half of the nineteenth century but a "likeness" in which some of the features of Victorian Peterhead are highlighted.

"PRACTISERS OF THE POPULAR ART"

As far as is known, the first references in Peterhead to the practice of photography in the local area appeared in the advertising columns of the *Peterhead Sentinel* on 4th September, 1857, when two itinerant professional photographers and a local amateur coincidentally announced their intention of taking photographic portraits in the town.

Three weeks later, in highlighting their presence in Peterhead, the editor of the paper observed that "the lieges of our good town have abundant opportunities just now for getting their portraits taken, and that too, in the first style of the art. Messrs Miller & Jamieson, photographers from Edinburgh, are doing their endeavours, with much success, to show their customers in their true light, as will be seen by their numerous specimens in the booksellers' windows. As their stay is to be limited, those who intend paying them a visit, to secure the shadow ere the substance is faded, should do so immediately. Mr Beaton, teacher, Rora, is also sojourning amongst us, taking likenesses by the same process (collodion) and has produced some first class portraits." Mr Beaton donated the profits from his photographic sessions for the improvement of the school at Rora and repeated the project in the following year. This surely qualified him for inclusion in the *Guinness Book of Records* as the first teacher to take photographs in aid of a school's "Building Fund"! (When Mr. Beaton retired, "at the harvest vacation", in 1874, the parochial School Board voted him an annual pension of £30.)

During the first three weeks of their visit to Peterhead, Miller and Jamieson were "taking their first-class portraits at Mrs. Henry's, Society Close, Broad Place," but moved to "Mr. Henderson's, foot of Broad Street" for the last two weeks. Mr. Beaton, meanwhile, was at work in Broad Place Pavilion.

The temporary nature of the tenancies of these improvised "photographic rooms", by both locally-based and itinerant artists of the lens, was demonstrated when, at the end of October, the *Sentinel* drew attention to the increasing number of *practisers of the popular art.* "Not long since," it reported, "the word which is now in everybody's mouth was the next thing to unknown and now, moreover, not only is every one getting his photograph, but every one seems to be turning photographer. Mr. Gregory has commenced in the Broad Place Pavilion; Mr Milne, we hear, is trying the art in Society Close; Mr Shivas has been for some time producing excellent portraits in Jamaica Street; and last, but far from least, our ingenious friend, Mr Henderson, has been showing the light and shade of the human physiognomy with admirable skill, and

sending out pictures which might do honour to one who has had far more experience. We have before us a collection of portraits taken by Mr Henderson, which at least have this recommendation - they are faithful representations of the originals - and, as pictures, some of his efforts are very good. Courteous reader, if you have not yet got your portrait, we would advise you to embrace the first opportunity - to wit, a fine day - and be off to the photographer."

Even allowing for editorial exaggeration, it seems that "photomania", which was then sweeping the country, had reached Peterhead. In the space of two months - September and October, 1857 - seven photographers advertised their intention of taking photographic portraits in the town.

The editor did not remind his readers that Mr. Gregory, who still called himself an "Artist", had been working in Peterhead nine months earlier. On that occasion, when he was willing to clean old paintings and re-gild picture frames as well as to paint portraits, there was no mention of photography. The absence of editorial comment on the re-appearance of a portrait-painter as a portrait-photographer using the collodion process suggests that his readers already accepted the camera as a replacement for the brush and palette in the quick and relatively cheap production of photographic portraits or "likenesses". Similar metamorphoses were taking place all over the country. In 1851, for example, the Aberdeen-based portrait miniaturist, George Washington Wilson, was conducting "Private Classes for Drawing and Painting"; by 1858, he was a well-established professional photographer winning widespread acclaim for the prints he submitted for exhibition in London.

Mr. Gregory intimated that he had "received FIRST CLASS APPARATUS by which he is enabled to execute portraits in the best style of the art, from one shilling (5p) upwards." A month earlier, when Messrs Miller and Jamieson claimed that their photographic portraits were unsurpassed "for artistic arrangement, natural colouring, pleasing expression, clearness, distinctness and undoubted truthfulness" and were better than "the most finished miniature paintings and at a cost most trifling", they were emphasising the fact that the collodion process had sounded the death-knell of the painters of miniatures. Few would pay from £10 to £20 for a miniature when a good photographic portrait was available for a matter of shillings!

At the end of October, 1857, Messrs Henderson and Shivas announced that they had "entered into partnership for the various branches of Photography, namely, SINGLE PORTRAITS, FAMILY GROUPS, RURAL SCENES, STREETS, SHIPS, etc. etc." at their Photographic Establishment, 41 Broad Street, where they had fitted up an elegant Waiting Room and were using the best instruments and materials that could be procured. The quality of the natural light of the sun was the main factor in determining when a photograph could be taken and so November was not the most propitious month in which to launch such an ambitious extension of the "various branches of Photography". The partnership seems to have been short-lived. In January, 1858, Henderson advertised that he was taking portraits "every lawful day from Ten till dusk" in his Photographic Establishment at 41, Foot of Broad Street. Less than two months later, Shivas spent two weeks at "Miss Henry's, in Longside," taking "Portraits for Lockets etc." and in June, 1858, he announced he would be "taking portraits professionally for a short time at the premises belonging to Mr. J. Anderson, Cabinetmaker, Mid Street, Fraserburgh." After seeing specimens of his work, the editor of the *Fraserburgh Advertiser* commented that Mr. James Shivas was "a young artist, who, by careful application, will no doubt succeed in his profession", a forecast which was completely substantiated by the photographer's subsequent career, which is outlined in a separate chapter.

In January, 1858, the *Peterhead Sentinel* reported, "We have had another addition to our Photographic Artists. Mr. J. Stuart from Edinburgh has fitted up convenient premises in Broad Place and is successfully prosecuting the beautiful art. The specimens of his workmanship which we have seen are done in a high style of art and cannot but draw the notice of those who like to see the actual facsimile of themselves. As an instance of the power of the lenses used by Mr. Stuart we may mention that we have seen the first page of last week's *Sentinel* taken on glass so distinctly that every word could have been read. This "fresh blood" will doubtless induce some to get another likeness and those who have not yet done so to "come out", and be at the same time a stimulus to our local artists. Nothing like competition."

Stuart claimed to have "over five years' experience in the first establishments in Edinburgh and New York" and intimated that he was about to open an Establishment in Aberdeen. The authenticity of his *curriculum vitae* has to be taken at face value; he did not, of course, produce any evidence of his experience in New York and Edinburgh and nothing is known of any establishment he may have opened in Aberdeen. For the limited period he was working in Peterhead, he erected a "suitable Pavilion, with Waiting- and Dressing-room attached, in Broad Place, next door to the *Sentinel* office." Using apparatus by eminent makers, including Ross of London, he pronounced his readiness to "produce Life-like Likenesses, in groups or otherwise, in a few seconds in any weather, on Glass or Paper, Coloured in the highest style of art, and which for truthfulness, durability, and beauty of finish are second to none." He presented himself as the complete photographer, skilled in taking "Views, Residences, and Portraits for Brooches, Lockets, etc. and in copying accurately pictures and other works of art." Those "wishing portraits for friends abroad," he announced, "can have them taken on card so as to be enclosed in a letter. Any number from one sitting." His prices were from two shillings and sixpence (12½p) upward. By the end of the first week in March, Stuart had moved to 35, Queen Street, where, for the next two weeks, he continued taking portraits "in all styles of Art, on Plate, Glass, and Paper, in all weathers, from ten a.m. till dusk." Appealing unashamedly to the sentimentality which characterised the Victorian age, he promoted his portraits as everlasting momentoes of absent friends, alive or dead.

Friends may mix with kindred clay,
But Stuart's portraits don't decay;
Lack they nothing but the breath,
Youth preservers from old death;
Stand they forth in living bloom,
Faithful pictures round my room;
Dewy tear-drops cloud my view,
As I scan these portraits true;
Distant though my friends may be,
Here their faces I can see;
See the bloom upon the cheek,
Fancy oft I hear them speak,
Gaze upon the lips which I
Oft have pressed in ecstacy;
See the very face I prize,
Looking at me with bright eyes;
Truthful pictures chaste and rife
Stuart's process mimics life;
Fadeless in their beauteous hue,
Like the heavens pellucid blue
Friends shall fade and drop through time,
Stuart's portraits keep their prime.

While portrait photography continued to be the main source of income of local "practisers of the popular art", better equipment and new techniques enabled the leading international photographers to produce prints which led one Victorian commentator to observe, "Photography is essentially the poor man's art; by it he becomes a traveller and a critic." Copies of the masterpieces of the great classical artists and scenic and architectural "views" were produced with an eye not only on their market value but also on the possibility of their inclusion in the exhibitions which were becoming regular features in the art lovers' calendar.

In April, 1858, W.L.Taylor, an enterprising local bookseller and newsagent, "respectfully invited attention to a selection of photographs" which were to be on view for eight days in his shop. Readers of the *Sentinel* were informed that "Several of these are the productions of French artists and others are from the master hand of Fenton, whose Crimean photographs are so justly admired. Of the French specimens, those representing some of the principal buildings in Paris display to perfection the elaborate decorations and fine statuary of these splendid erections. Fenton's views are mostly Highland scenery, and of these the most remarkable are Balmoral Castle and a scene at Castleton of Braemar. There are also some copies of the paintings of the old Italian masters."

Photographs by Roger Fenton and the French photographer, Gustav Le Gray, were included in the first exhibition arranged in Edinburgh by the Photographic Society of Scotland in December, 1856, and also in the Exhibition of the Art Treasures of the United Kingdom which opened in Manchester in May, 1857. Advertisements in the *Aberdeen Herald* informed readers that a Registry of Apartments - a list of accommodation available in private houses for paying guests - had been compiled for the convenience of visitors to the Manchester Exhibition. The importance of the expanding railway network in the promotion of such exhibitions is well illustrated by the arrangements by the Scottish North-Eastern Railway for a "Cheap Train". (For the visit to Manchester at a fare of 32s.6d (£1.63) return, passengers from Aberdeen travelled to Perth during the afternoon of Thursday, 25th June, and joined the 9.15 a.m. train for Manchester on Friday morning. For their return journey, they left Manchester at 5 p.m. on Monday, 29th June, and arrived in Perth in time to join the train for Aberdeen at 6 o'clock on Tuesday morning.) While Mr. Taylor would have been fully aware of these arrangements, we have no way of knowing whether he visited the exhibition. It seems likely, however, that he had managed to acquire copies of some of the prints on view there, including a selection from the series of Scottish subjects by Roger Fenton, for display in Peterhead.

Commenting on this, the first photographic exhibition in the town, the *Sentinel* pronounced, "It is no disparagement to native talent to say that they are the finest specimens of the art we ever saw.....To the lovers of the fine arts in Peterhead, seldom is such a treat afforded." There is no record of how "the lovers of the fine arts" reacted but the high standard of the prints on view, attainable by only the most proficient professionals, certainly did not discourage aspiring "native talent" from trying their hand at the "beautiful art". The majority of the newcomers regarded their venturing into the photographic world as a novel side-line and did not commit themselves on a full-time basis. Inexperienced and comparatively unskilled as they were, most of them had relatively short careers as portrait photographers and no examples of their work have been identified.

In July, 1858, George Fraser erected a "Photographic Portrait Gallery" at 30, Harbour Street, where he could "take portraits in any kind of weather and at very moderate prices."

In January, 1859, William Milne, a native of Peterhead, erected a "GLASSHOUSE" at 12, Broad Street, where he produced photographic portraits "on GLASS or PAPER, in the dullest weather." He also took "Stereoscopic Portraits or Views by the calotype process in the first style and at moderate charges." Having acquired "all the latest improvements", he was able to dispense with his older equipment. His "FOR SALE" advertisement, in February, 1859, of "a LENS for PORTRAITS, 4 by 5 inches, and a LENS for VIEWS, 5 by 6 inches", with Mahogany Camera, and Dipping Bath, gives some idea of a photographer's basic equipment. According to the census in 1861, aged 38, he was still working as a photographer at 12, Broad Street.

A year later, in February, 1860, William Herd, who advertised himself as "previously and still engaged in House, Sign, and Ship Painting", entered the photographic business when he "erected a new, elegant, and commodious GLASS HOUSE suitable for Photographic purposes" at 40, Broad Street, where, with instruments made by the most celebrated makers of the day, he promised to produce "LIKENESSES of a Superior Quality" at prices of one shilling (5p) and upwards .

In March, 1861, Mr. Nisbet "begged to intimate that, at his PHOTOGRAPHIC ESTABLISHMENT in Queen Street, Portraits are carefully taken on the most approved principle from Sixpence (2½p) upward." The *Sentinel*, ever ready to promote the work of portrait photographers, drew attention to the fact that "Mr. Nisbet, the celebrated photographic artist, is still prolonging his stay here. His frank and easy way of doing his work and a thorough knowledge of photographic chemistry and optics all tend to enable him to produce what is wanted - a good likeness. We would recommend all those who wish their portraits to pay a visit to his establishment as the specimens we have seen are first class, and the truthfulness is second to none, and the prices are within the reach of everyone." The itinerant "Mr. Nisbet", who was working in a temporary studio at 19, Queen Street, was presumably one of two brothers, Thomas and William, who were recorded in the 1861 Census as photographers from Larbert, Stirling, who were lodging at 17, Queen Street, Peterhead.

Two months later, in May, 1861, Joseph Collier "fitted up a neat GLASS-HOUSE in Mr. Creighton's Timber-yard, head of Queen Street", where he set about producing calotypes and stereoscopic portraits of a very high standard. An account of Collier's career is given in a later chapter.

Some idea of the "glass houses", in which many photographers worked at this time, may be gathered from an advertisement which appeared in the *Fraserburgh Advertiser* in September, 1862. "For Sale A Glass House suitable for a florist etc. 15½ft. by 7ft.9ins. Upset price £7." The photographer, who had furnished new "Portrait Rooms" and was disposing of his former "studio", suggested that "Owing to the construction, it could be cut so as to make two neat Green Houses each 7½ft. square, thus suiting two parties at a mere trifling expense."

In July, 1866, George Cruickshank announced that he had "succeeded Mr. James Shivas in that comfortably fitted up STUDIO, No.59 BROAD STREET, where, with instruments by the best makers and careful manipulation on his own part, he will endeavour to produce PHOTOGRAPHS of a FIRST CLASS CHARACTER". Cruickshank's main business enterprise at 59, Broad Street, was his "Fancy Warehouse" where he sold a "well-selected Stock of FANCY GOODS, among which will be found a complete assortment of JEWELLERY, CUTLERY, POCKET BOOKS, PORTMONIES, STATIONERY, CONCERTINAS, FLUTES and other musical instruments etc. Violin strings of the best make. To all smokers of the social weed, G. C. would strongly recommend a trial of his BOGGIE ROLL, VIRGINIA AND IRISH ROLL, CAVENDISH etc. In CIGARS, he has always a fresh supply of Conchas, Regalia, Reyna, Havannah, and Cubans etc. etc. Every article in connection with the tobacco trade kept in stock PIPES, TOBACCO POUCHES, and SNUFF BOXES in great variety." Initially, at least, George Cruickshank was ready to invest further in photography, which he obviously regarded as a potentially lucrative second string to his bow. In 1867, he "added much that is new and essential to the production of high-class Pictures" and in 1868, "having refitted his Photographic Room, he was now in a position to take First-Class Likenesses." His sojourn in the photographic world, however, was short-lived.

In March, 1870, John Robertson "commenced the business of PHOTOGRAPHER in the Gallery situated at 59½, BROAD STREET (lately occupied by Mr. G. Cruickshank)". This seems to have been Robertson's first venture as a professional photographer. (He was a merchant tailor in Cultercullen, Foveran, when he was married in 1865; in the 1871 census, he was recorded as a photographer residing at 3, Merchant Street, Peterhead; when he registered the birth of his third son the following year, he was still a photographer but was living in West Street, Strichen; and by the end of the decade, no longer a full-time professional photographer, he had left the district and was living in Aberdeen.) When in Peterhead, he was keen to merit a share of public support and assured potential patrons that "No expense has been spared in providing instruments of the newest and most perfect construction while alterations have been effected to the Gallery, both of which will be found beneficial in the further and more successful development of the Art." He reduced his charges; in September, 1870, he published photographs of the Obelisk in the New Cemetery at a price of sixpence (2½p) each and, in January, 1872, he was selling his *cartes de visite* at four shillings (20p) per dozen.

At that time, James Thom, Photographer, 28, Maiden Street, was charging six shillings (30p) per dozen for his *cartes de visite*. Four years earlier, in January, 1868, he had announced "that, having resolved to devote a larger portion of his time to PHOTOGRAPHY than he has hitherto done, he has just fitted up a handsome and commodious suite of Rooms at 28, Maiden Street, where he will have every facility for carrying on the business in all its departments." Thom, who ran the Peterhead Dye Works at the same address, continued, "J.T. having been for about four years under the tuition of Mr. J. Collier, late of Peterhead (whose artistic abilities have been acknowledged wherever his Pictures have been seen) and by possessing himself of FIRST CLASS instruments and the newest chemical appliances, hopes to be able to produce Pictures which will give every satisfaction to those kind enough to patronise him." He produced portraits from Locket-size to 12 by 15 inches and was willing to photograph "Gentlemen's Country Residences, Landscapes, and other Out-door Views." In March, 1869, the *Sentinel* drew attention to "the interesting copies made by Mr. Thom, from a very scarce, old, but beautiful print of His Excellency Field Marshal Keith, C.-in-C. of His Prussian Majesty's Forces in Germany. Both the *carte* and large-plate size are successful copies and, to lovers of the Keith family, are worth the purchase price." Five months later, Thom took photographs during the unveiling of the statue of Field Marshal Keith in Broad Street.

To ensure that his pictures could stand comparison with any produced in the district, he renewed his equipment regularly. In 1872, for example, "to keep to the age with the improvements constantly being made in the practice of Photography", Thom purchased some of the newest and most approved apparatus in quick-acting powerful lenses and other accessories, some of which were specially adapted for photographing children.

In May, 1877, still carrying on business as a dyer as well as a photographer, Thom begged "to intimate his Removal from 28 Maiden Street to New and Commodious Premises, No.11 Erroll Street, where he will continue to attend to all orders entrusted to his care." Three years later, he was no longer personally active in the photographic side of the business for on 28th April, 1880, Mr. H. Gordon, Photographic Artist, 3 Belmont Street, Aberdeen, announced that he would be at Mr. Thom's Photographic Studio, Erroll Street, Peterhead, on Wednesday, Thursday, Friday, and Saturday every week. In May, 1882, Gordon returned "his best thanks to his many Friends and Customers in Peterhead and District for the liberal patronage awarded him since his first visit among them" and intimated that he had again opened his studio for the practice of his art for the summer. His advertisement continued, "H.G having made a special study of Landscape Photography is in a position to execute all orders entrusted to his care in the Highest Style of Art and at the lowest Charges consistent with Careful and Artistic Workmanship. Specimens of Portraits and Landscapes may be seen and Prices learned by calling at the PETERHEAD PHOTOGRAPHIC STUDIO, ERROLL STREET."

Gordon's "business plan" must have been suddenly and drastically altered for, on 14th June, 1882, John Logan, "Photographic Artist From St. Andrews, Successor to Mr.H. Gordon" took the "opportunity of informing the Nobility and Gentry and Public generally that he has bought and is now carrying on the PHOTOGRAPHIC BUSINESS belonging to Mr. H. Gordon, Peterhead; and trusts that from his long experience in the Photographic Art and by strict personal attention to Business to merit a liberal share of the public support. Mr. Logan had the honour to photograph H.R.H. the Duke of Edinburgh; also H.R.H. Prince Leopold, in St. Andrews. First Class *Cartes de Visite* 6s (30p) per doz.; Cabinets 12s (60p) per doz.; Groups etc. by arrangements. All kinds of outdoor Photographing done on shortest notice. American Gem Photographs 9 for 1s (5p) finished in a few minutes. Customers get supplied before leaving. Studio open daily from 9 a.m. to 7 p.m."

Before moving to Peterhead, John Logan had his own studio in St. Andrews but he may have been economic of the truth regarding the royal photographs. The Duke of Edinburgh and Prince Leopold, the fourth son of Queen Victoria, had been photographed in St. Andrews, the former in 1871 and the latter in 1876. Both photographs were taken in a studio run by Thomas Rodger, who had been trained by Dr. John Adamson, the first calotypist in Scotland. It is not certain, therefore, if John Logan took the royal photographs but he could have been an assistant or apprentice in Rodger's studio at the time. If this was the case, Logan would have received an excellent grounding as a practical photographer but there is no extant evidence of the quantity or quality of the portraits or outdoor prints he produced while in Peterhead; nor is anything known of his American Gem Photographs.

B1 *East side of Thistle Street, Peterhead, before demolition and rebuilding prior to 1888. Photograph by William Robertson.*

B2 Reverse of carte de visite by Wm. Robertson.

In April, 1886, William Robertson, a native of Oldmeldrum, took the "opportunity of thanking his many friends and customers for the liberal patronage bestowed on him since he commenced business in Peterhead" and intimated that he had moved to a new and commodious studio at 3, Queen Street. He offered to supply "One dozen Finely Mounted *Cartes* for 6s (30p) or One dozen ditto with one Cabinet Size for 7s6d (37½p)." By June, 1887, his address was 5, Queen Street. Four years later, he was advertising copyright views of the *Convict Prison* and of the *Laying of the Foundation Stone, Peterhead Free Library*, from 6d (2½p) up to 2s. (10p).

On 1st September, 1886, Grant and Officer announced that they had "opened the PHOTOGRAPHIC STUDIO, 32 ERROLL STREET, where visitors will be attended to daily between the hours of 10 a.m. and 4 p.m.". In April the following year, they reduced the prices of their photographic portraits - for example, *carte* size were 6s.6d, (32½p) per dozen - and announced their readiness to copy old or faded photographs and to undertake outside work.

In 1890, T. W. Grant was advertising his photographic business based in 32, Erroll Street and also at 2, York Street.

A similar advertisement appeared in 1891 but Grant was not listed as a photographer living in Peterhead in the decennial census which was carried out that year. Only William Robertson, James Shivas, and Thomas Hutchison were recorded as photographers and employers. Fred Shivas, the sixteen-year old son of James, was a photographer's assistant and presumably worked with his father. One photographer, one assistant photographer, and two photographic printers were also listed in the 1891 census; they were not classed as employers and no indication was given as to their respective employers. Ten years previously, James Shivas was the only photographer in Peterhead who was described as an employer; he had two men and three girls on his staff. At that time, the enumerators who collected the data for the census specifically identified only three residents in the town who were employed in photography - one photographic artist, one photographic printer, and one albumen maker! Some of those employed in photography may have lived outwith the census area and some may have been employed on a part-time basis. This was certainly the case in 1871. Apart from two photographers - James Shivas and John Robertson - only one person, a photographer's shopwoman, was identified as having any connection with the photographic business; even James Thom, who ran his own studio for about twelve years after working as an assistant to Joseph Collier, was not identified as a photographer but as a dyer!

Of all those who had tried their hand at the "beautiful art" in the Peterhead area, James Shivas, the town's artist of the lens *par excellence*, was the only one who, having committed himself on a full-time basis in the early pioneering days, was still active at the beginning of the twentieth century. As might be expected, his photographs feature prominently in *A PETERHEAD PORTRAIT* but material from less predictable sources is also available.

For example, his friend and companion on his daily morning constitutional, W. L. Taylor, whose career as a bookseller in the town spanned the second half of the nineteenth century, published the first series of stereoscopic views of the town and vicinity.

TOWN OF PETERHEAD,

Respectfully Dedicated to the Provost, Magistrates and Council of Peterhead.

C1 Lithograph by C. J. Greenwood; published by William L. Taylor.

WILLIAM L. TAYLOR : *PETERHEAD AND ITS ENVIRONS IN STEREOSCOPE*

William L.Taylor was born on 18th July, 1829, in the parish of King Edward, Aberdeenshire. After attending the parish school at New Byth, he was employed by Lewis Smith, Publisher, Aberdeen, and then canvassed books around New Byth for a brief period before moving to Peterhead to work as an assistant with Messrs Mudie, Booksellers, St. Andrew Street. On 18th March, 1851, he announced in the *Banffshire Journal* that he had opened a new "Bookbinding Bookselling and Stationery Warehouse" in Peterhead "in that Shop immediately under FRASER'S INN, BROAD STREET, and trusts that, from his long acquaintance with the Trade, and commencing with an *Entirely* NEW STOCK, *personally* selected, he will be able to supply those who may favour him with their orders in a satisfactory manner, with the utmost promptitude, and on the very best terms. W.L.T. has always on hand a supply of MERCHANTS' ACCOUNT BOOKS, DAY-BOOKS, JOURNALS, LEDGERS, of a great variety of sizes, and will Bind and Rule to any pattern, on the shortest notice. All the London and Edinburgh PERIODICALS supplied as published. Books bound to pattern".

Previously occupied by James Skinner, hat manufacturer, the shop in which he set up business was one of three on the ground floor of The Inn, on the site of the present Royal Hotel. In July, 1852, The Inn was completely destroyed by fire. When the premises were re-built, Taylor again leased a shop on the site - on Broad Street, at the pend leading to Broadplace - and occupied it until his death in 1910.

His new premises were advertised in the *Banffshire Journal*, on 30th May 1854, and he announced that he had published two views of the town, *C1 Peterhead From the Sea* and *C3 Town of Peterhead.* Drawn and lithographed by C.J. Greenwood in 1852, they were "Respectfully Dedicated to the Provost, Magistrates and Council of Peterhead". Clearly visible on the horizon, on the left of the former view - reproduced on page 14 - is the Meethill monument, which had been erected by the local Whigs to commemorate the passing of the 1832 Reform Act; on the horizon towards the right side is the tower of the windmill, which used to stand on the knoll at Balmoor. An early, sail-assisted steamship is featured among the vessels in the bay in the other view which, drawn from a point near the Invernettie brickwork, appears overleaf .

Taylor published another lithograph of Peterhead, which pre-dates both the views featured above. At the right of the picture, on the seaward side of the Keith Inch, there is a windmill which, by the time the other two lithographs were drawn, had been dismantled by its owner, Alexander Murray of Blackhouse, who used the stones from the ruin for some building work at the Kirkburn Mills, where he ran a saw-mill, a flour and meal mill, and a bone crushing establishment.

This lithograph was drawn by Mary Forbes, whose grandfather, William Forbes, was manager of the Invernettie brickwork from about 1801 until he died in 1837, the period during which the output of tiles,

C2 William L.Taylor at the door of his shop in Broad Street, Peterhead.

PETERHEAD FROM THE SEA

Respectfully Dedicated to the Provost, Magistrates and Council of Peterhead.

C3 Lithograph by C. J. Greenwood; published by William L. Taylor.

pipes, and bricks reached a peak. After William Forbes died, the house adjoining the brickwork was occupied by this son, John, and family, including Mary, for whom the view across the bay, as reproduced below, would have been a familiar sight.

enterprise and acumen which were to be the hallmarks of his entire career. He arranged for a weekly parcel to be delivered from London and so periodicals, sheet music, and books could be supplied promptly. This enabled him to increase the stock of

C4 Lithograph by Mary Forbes; published by William L. Taylor.

She was obviously a gifted artist who, presumably, had inherited the talent from her father, a professional artist. (John Forbes had a brief but promising career as a portrait painter in London until he had to return to Scotland for health reasons. Before moving to the brickwork, he had a brief spell in Inverness and lived for six years in Aberdeen, where he gave lessons to young professional and amateur painters. One of this pupils was John Phillip, who became a Royal Academician known for his paintings of characteristically Scottish scenes and for his more flamboyant canvases produced during the period he spent in Spain; as a result, he was given nicknames - *The Scottish Velasquez* or *Spanish Phillip*. Mary Forbes emigrated to America, around 1857, with her father, who resumed his career as a portrait painter in Kalamazoo, Chicago - where many of his finest paintings were destroyed in the *Great Fire* in October, 1871 - and Indianapolis.)

By publishing these lithographs before there were any photographic views of the area, when he was only twenty-four years old, W. L. Taylor displayed the

the Lending Library, which he had established in one part of his shop, with new and popular books soon after they were published. By his frequent advertisements in the *Sentinel*, he made sure that the public of Peterhead had ample opportunity to keep-up-to-date with their preferred reading. On 14th October, 1859, for example, he announced, "*Adam Bede*; *The Virginians* by Thackeray; Ellis's *Three Visits to Madagascar*; Carlyle's *Frederick The Great*; *Mignonette*; *The Curate and The Rector*; *The Man of Fortune*; and other new books have been added to W. L. Taylor's Library, Peterhead." (*Adam Bede* was published in 1859; *The Virginians* appeared in serial form, between November, 1857, and September, 1859; and *Frederick The Great* was published between 1858 and 1867.)

When Taylor first entered the trade, his stock of newspapers consisted of two Aberdeen weeklies. During the Crimean War, he and three friends combined to subscribe to *The Times*. It was carried from London to Aberdeen by train and then by mail coach to Peterhead, where it arrived on the afternoon of the day after which it had been printed. On 8th May, 1857, the *Sentinel* carried the following advertisement, "*THE TIMES*. For sale, a copy of *The Times* on third day after publication, delivered free in town, daily. Apply to W.L.Taylor". (Was this the paper that he and his three friends had previously read?!) Four years later, before the extension of the railway northward from Aberdeen reached Peterhead, he was employing one assistant and supplying some national papers - *Daily Scotsman, Edinburgh Courant, Caledonian Mercury,* and *Daily Review* - "every evening at seven o'clock at One Penny each, or seven shillings per quarter, paid in advance, delivered free in town". In the 1870s, his stock included golf clubs and balls and, by the 1880s, his staff had increased to an assistant and two boys.

W. L. Taylor was a kenspeckle figure in the town, recognisable by his tall hat, which he often wore behind the counter as well as in the street! The extent of his contribution to improving the quality of life in Peterhead may be gauged from the number and variety of his voluntary activities. He was Depute Chairman of the Feuars' Managers and Convener of their Education Committee; a Deacon in the Congregational Church; for forty years, a Director of the Peterhead Savings Bank; the treasurer of the Peterhead Reading Society; the organiser of the Sunday Free Meals Scheme which was supported entirely by voluntary contributions; for many years, the superintendent of the leaving certificate examinations in the local Academy; an active supporter of the town's Public Library to which he donated many books; and the President of the Buchan Field Club in 1900.

He had a life-long interest in books, which was fostered by Lewis Smith, his employer during his time in Aberdeen. When only seventeen years old, he became interested in the different versions of the Psalms and began to collect psalters - English, French, and Latin, as well as Scots. In spite of the comparative remoteness of Peterhead from the auction houses which usually handled such rare items and with only a very limited budget at his disposal, Taylor assembled a unique psalmody collection, including John Knox's *Book of Common Prayer*, with the *Geneva Psalter* attached, and a prayer-book, with *King James's Psalms* attached - the same as the book Jenny Geddes is said to have thrown during her protest against episcopacy in St. Giles Cathedral, Edinburgh, in July, 1637. He also collected many other scarce volumes. Among his collectors' items was a copy of the *Geneva Bible*, which was printed in Geneva in 1560 and came to be known as the *Breeches Bible* on account of Genesis chapter 3, verse 7 - "they sewed fig leaves together and made themselves breeches." (*The Authorized Version* says, "they sewed fig leaves together and made themselves

aprons." *The New English Bible* says, "they stitched fig-leaves together and made themselves loincloths.") He also had a copy of the *Bishops' Bible*, published in 1568 and later known as the *Treacle Bible* because of Jeremiah chapter 8, verse 22 - "Is there no treacle in Gilead.....?" (*The Authorized Version* and *The New English Bible* both say, "Is there no balm in Gilead.....?")

Eight months after Taylor died on 11th April, 1910, a large part of his collection of books went under the hammer in Dowell's Auction Room in George Street, Edinburgh. On the first day of the sale, one of the earliest printed copies of Barbour's *Brus* was sold for five shillings (25p) and Blind Harry's *Wallace* went for fourteen shillings and sixpence (72p).

His psalters were not dispersed and the *William Lawrence Taylor Collection* is now preserved in Aberdeen University's *Special Collections and Archives* in King's College. The variety of the items in the Taylor Collection is illustrated in *C5*, reproduced on page 19. At the top left, containing "manie Godlie Prayers, as well for Morning as Evening, as also before and after SERMONS, and the Holie COMMUNION, and for every person : with a perfect Table of the Psalms" is a copy of *The CL PSALMES Of the Princelie Prophet David, in ENGLISH METRE, According as they are sung in the CHURCH OF SCOTLAND*. This book of one hundred and fifty psalms was printed, in 1629, by Edward Raban - the first printer in Aberdeen - "for David Melvill", the city's first bookseller; hence the *Bon Accord* coat of arms on the title page. To the right of the *PSALMES*, is a page of music, with one of the full-page illustrations, from *Harmonia Sacra*, a very early tune-book for sacred music. At the bottom right, is the title page of the oldest item in the collection. Printed in Venice, in 1502, it is an extremely rare book by Cardinal Turrecremata, an eminent theologian. The other two illustrations are from the Second Edition of *HYMNS ADAPTED TO THE CHURCH SERVICES THROUGHOUT THE CHRISTIAN YEAR : With a Selection of Metrical Psalms*, which was published in Peterhead, in 1860, by W.L.Taylor; the First Edition appeared in 1857 and a Third Edition was published in 1866. The *Second Paraphrase*, beginning "O God of Bethel! by whose hand", appears as No. 24, suitable for Evening Worship, while No. 25, beginning "Creator of the starry poles!" is recommended for Advent. (This psalter was compiled by the Rev. Dr. Gilbert Rorison, incumbent of St. Peter's Scottish Episcopal Church, Peterhead, from 1845 until his death in 1869.)

While gathering his collection of psalters, Taylor became an expert in psalmody and, in a typically Victorian evening's entertainment in February, 1886, he delivered a lecture in the Congregational Church,

C5 *From the William L. Taylor Collection in King's College, Aberdeen.*

Peterhead, on *The History of the Metrical Psalms from their Introduction into Scotland in 1564 to 1781*. The lecture was illustrated by a quartette singing ancient versions of the psalms to their original tunes and the proceeds from the sale of tickets, at sixpence (2½p) each, were donated to a charitable organisation associated with the Church.

He became a member of the Bibliographical Society of Edinburgh and compiled a *Bibliography of Peterhead Literature : 1593-1900*, in which he is named as the publisher of a considerable number of sermons, poems, and books of local interest including *The Life of Rev. John Skinner, Author of Tullochgorum, with his Songs and Poems* by Sir H. G.Reid; and *Old Inverugie and its Associations - Social, Domestic and Political* by William Boyd.

The fast-growing photographic industry presented him with further business opportunities. As described previously, he exhibited the works of internationally known photographers and was always willing to display and retail the photographs produced by local "practisers of the popular art". In his later years, which coincided with the postcard-collecting mania of the 1890s and early 1900s, Taylor arranged for cards carrying his imprint to be produced as, for example, on this view of Peterhead Academy, *C6*.

concentrated on the more popular tourist haunts on the continent as well as in Britain. In September, 1854, for example, A. Rae, the Banff chemist and part-time daguerreotypist, announced that he "had got to hand... a quantity of stereoscopic views, principally Parisian, from 2 shillings (10p) a slide" and, in the first week of January, 1857, Hay and Lyall, Opticians, Market Street, Aberdeen, advertised a "great variety of transparent and paper views in Switzerland, the Pyrenees, Rome, Florence, Vienna, Milan, and Paris." At the same time, they offered views of "the Isle of Wight, Edinburgh, Aberdeen, Deeside, Elgin, Forfarshire, etc.".

These advertisements did not specify the views nor did they identify the photographers who had produced them but George Washington Wilson, aware of the potential of this burgeoning market, began taking scenic stereographs in 1855, when copies of his *Old Mill at Cults* were sold at 2 shillings (10p) each. Soon afterwards, possibly in 1856, he issued his first list of forty-four stereoscopic views of Aberdeen, Deeside, and Elgin.

During the stereomania of the 1850s and 1860s, a stereoscope and a selection of stereoscopic photographs were the technological parallels of the television set and camcorder of the late twentieth

New Academy Schools, Peterhead.

C6 Peterhead Academy.

His most enterprising contribution to the creation of a photographic archive of Victorian Peterhead, however, was as publisher of two series of topographical stereographs entitled, *PETERHEAD AND ITS ENVIRONS IN STEREOSCOPE*.

The mass-production of stereoscopic slides required considerable investment of labour and capital. Photographers, working on the assumption that views of places which attracted visitors would sell readily,

century. With a selection of these mass-produced topographical slides, the ordinary man-in-the-street could, through the medium of the stereoscope, become a stay-at-home tourist! It is not surprising, therefore, that several shopkeepers in Peterhead were advertising stereoscopes, priced from three shillings (15p) to three pounds, with stocks of stereographs, which were not identified by name. It may be assumed, however, on the evidence of the following examples, from the slides still extant in the Arbuthnot

Museum, that stereoscopic views similar to those advertised in Aberdeen were available locally.

*C7 **Brig o' Balgownie**,* above, was photographed by George Washington Wilson. The photographers responsible for the others have not been identified and only in the case of *C8 **Ballater on the Dee**,* below, has the retailer been named; he was Andrew Elliot, Bookseller and Stationer, 15 Princes Street, Edinburgh.

unequalled for picturesque beauty and grandeur", was printed on a label on the back of *C9 **Edinburgh From Calton Hill**,* below.

In *C10 **Princes Street from East Princes Street Gardens**,* above, the view of one of the city's main tourist attractions, the monument erected in honour of Sir Walter Scott in 1846, was expected to boost sales.

Some publishers of stereographs supplied information to help viewers to set the slides in context. For example, "Edinburgh, the metropolis of Scotland is situated about a mile and a half from the Frith (sic) of Forth and extends to about two miles in length and breadth. It is built upon three elevated ridges, the Old Town occupying that in the centre and the New Town that on the north. The views from the elevated points of the city and the neighbourhood, such as from the Castle, the Calton Hill, and Arthur's Seat, are

The next two illustrations also show how tourism influenced the production of stereographs. The first, *C11 **View taken from the Steeple of St. Mark**,* was one of a series on Venice and showed one of the perennially most popular tourist attractions in Europe. The other, *C12 **Schoolhouse at Bonawe Ferry, Loch Etive**,* presumably owed its publication to the increasing interest in the Highlands, which was the result of Queen Victoria's well publicised passion for Balmoral. (George Washington Wilson capitalised on this; after taking photographs at Balmoral, he advertised himself as *Photographer To The Queen*.)

C13 Auld Lang Syne.

C11 View from the steeple of St. Mark.

C14 An Evening Meal.

C12 Schoolhouse, Bonawe.

Slides such as *C13 Auld Lang Syne*, *C14 An Evening Meal*, and *C15 Uncle Toby and Widow Wadman* - all now in the local collection - were also available. Presumably, viewers were informed that the final part of *The Life and Opinions of Tristram Shandy* by Laurence Sterne, which was published in nine volumes between 1760 and 1767, was concerned mainly with the love-affair of Uncle Toby, one of the main characters, and the Widow Wadman. Although the novel was considered worthy of translation into French and German, it was denounced on moral and literary grounds by Sterne's contemporaries, Dr. Samuel Johnson, Horace Walpole, and Oliver

C15 Uncle Toby and Widow Wadman.

Goldsmith. It is surprising, therefore, to find the two figures being featured - about a century after the appearance of the last volume of the novel - on a stereograph, which was, presumably, included in the"slide collection" of a mid-Victorian household!

Peterhead-based photographers, such as William Milne and James Shivas, were intimating their readiness to take stereoscopic portraits and views, if requested by customers. We have no information regarding the origin of the stereograph, *C16 In Collieston*, half of which is shown below but it could be the work of either of these local photographers.

C16 In Collieston : A fishing family is baiting sma' (small) lines, with mussels or limpets, preparatory to setting them, inshore, to try to catch white fish.

Neither Milne nor Shivas was equipped, however, nor had they the capital required to undertake the production on a commercially viable scale, on spec, of a large number of stereoscopic views. The appearance of a representative series of stereographs of the local area must, therefore, have seemed a very remote possibility at the time.

On 2nd September, 1859, however, William L.Taylor announced that "a series of upwards of twenty STEREOGRAPHS" of Peterhead and district would be ready the following week. When the series of views of "*PETERHEAD AND ITS ENVIRONS IN STEREOSCOPE*" was eventually published on 28th October, it consisted of forty-four stereographs costing one shilling and threepence (6½p) each in black and white or one shilling and sixpence (7½p) coloured. On 14th September, 1860, he advertised another series of twenty-one local stereographs at one shilling (5p) each and announced that the earlier series would be reduced to one shilling (5p) each. Copies of some of these slides are reproduced elsewhere in this book to provide contemporary illustrations relative to various topics. *C17 - C28*, which appear on pages 24 and 25, have been chosen to help to create a likeness of Peterhead and the surrounding area in 1859-60.

These stereographs were made by George Dawson, a professional photographer based in Bath. It is not known whether he first visited the Peterhead area at the express invitation of William L.Taylor or whether he had taken the pictures while on a photographic itinerary and had subsequently arranged for their publication by Taylor. When Dawson was appointed Lecturer on Photography in the Department of Applied Science and Engineering, King's College, London, readers of the *Sentinel* were informed, on 22nd November, 1861, that he was "well known in this quarter in connection with his stereoscopic views of the locality, published by Mr. W. L. Taylor." Dawson was described as "an accomplished scholar, a sound chemist, and a first-rate practical photographer, well fitted for the work he has undertaken" and was to be congratulated on "this well-merited appointment, the more so that he was the unanimous selection of the Council of the College over forty candidates." In spite of this glowing testimonial, Dawson was forced to leave the College, in 1879, after being reported for drinking and dereliction of duty! However, extant stereographs from his *Peterhead and Its Environs* series testify to his undoubted skill as a photographer; more importantly, due largely to the entrepreneurship of William L. Taylor, they have survived as the oldest dateable views of the Peterhead area.

C21 The Free Church. (Now the Trinity Church; the foreground is now the car park at the Palace Hotel.)

C22 The Town House, Peterhead.

C19 The Old Church, Peterhead.

C20 The Parish Church, Peterhead.

C17 Peterhead from the South.

C18 Peterhead from the old churchyard.

C27 *Rocks near Slains.*

C28 *Gateway to Inverugie Castle.*

C25 *The Earl of Aberdeen's Cottage (Earl's Lodge) with the ruins of Boddam Castle in the foreground.*

C26 *The front of Slains Castle.*

C23 *The South Harbour, Peterhead.*

C24 *The old harbour, Boddam.*

JOSEPH COLLIER : *THE HOWES O' BUCHAN*

Joseph Collier was born on 12th July, 1836, in the parish of King Edward, Aberdeenshire. In the 1841 Census, the Collier family was listed at Mains of Byth, King Edward, where Joseph's father was a merchant. Ten years later, his widowed mother was head of the family which then lived at Longhead of Auchnamoon, King Edward. She was described as a "Farmer of 60 acres, Grosser and Clothier, employing one labourer". Joseph was working on the farm, as were an elder brother and sister. In the next Census, in 1861, Joseph Collier was entered as a photographer, living at 14, North Street, Fraserburgh, with his wife Elsie, whom he had married on 19th November, 1860, in Aberdeen.

There is a persistent tradition among Collier's descendants that he was injured when working as a blacksmith. He is said to have read a book on photography while convalescing and this led him to embark on a career during which he came to be acknowledged as one of the leading artists of the lens on both sides of the Atlantic. Where or when he worked as a blacksmith is not known; nor has the inspirational book been identified. Collier used the calotype process in his early years as a professional photographer and so the stimulus may have been provided by Thomas Sutton's book, *The Calotype Process*, or John Rowland's *Photograph Manipulation : The Calotype and Collodion Processes*, both of which were published in 1855; or his interest in the "art-science" may have been kindled by *A Practical guide to the Collodion Process in Photography*, written in the same year by the Aberdeen photographer, George Washington Wilson.

In March, 1858, "The Art" was being taught "in all its branches" in at least one studio in Aberdeen - Lamb's Photographic Rooms, 19, George Street - and so Collier could have received some formal instruction from a professional photographer. There is no evidence of this and family lore asserts that he was self-taught, and that he and a future brother-in-law "experimented" in photography, using an old shed as a makeshift studio. This is highly probable for there seems to have been a very active interest in photography in the area around New Byth at the time, as was reflected in the significantly high number - including Collier's relations, the Browns and the Norries - who, having some family association with the district, later became professional photographers in various towns in the north-east.

By the time he was twenty-three years old, Joseph Collier had sufficient confidence in his own ability to insert the following advertisement in the *Fraserburgh Advertiser* on 27th April, 1860, "PHOTOGRAPHY J. COLLIER Respectfully intimates to the Inhabitants of Fraserburgh, and the surrounding Country, that he has commenced business at 16, North Street, where he is now producing PORTRAITS of a superior Style, on Glass, Paper, and Leather, at Prices ranging from one shilling (5p) and upwards. PHOTOGRAPHS SET IN BROOCHES, LOCKETS, ETC. PICTURES CAREFULLY COPIED. J.C. hopes with his excellent accommodation, moderate charges, and strict attention to business to obtain a part of Public Patronage."

In May, 1861, he moved to Peterhead, where he "fitted up a Neat GLASS-HOUSE in Mr. Creighton's Timber-yard, head of Queen Street." There, on the site now occupied by the Court House, he was ready to take "Calotype Portraits, 8 by 5 inches, to sizes fitted in Brooches, Lockets, or Rings. STEREOSCOPIC PORTRAITS, GROUPS, etc. on any day, whether wet or dry." He charged from one shilling (5p) to five shillings (25p) per photograph, according to size, and invited potential customers to inspect specimens "at the Photographic Rooms, Queen Street, or with Mr. W. L. Taylor, Bookseller, Broad Street."

The stereoscopic portrait, *D1 Lady with a Dog*, half of which is reproduced below, was presumably taken for a private individual, in Peterhead, and was not available for general retail sale. The photographer has not been identified but in view of the contemporaneous comments quoted in the following paragraph, it may be an example of Joseph Collier's work.

D1 Lady with a dog.

26

The siting of his "studio" in such inauspicious surroundings - a builder and timber merchant's yard - gave no hint of the standing which Collier would soon attain among his fellow professionals, but the *Sentinel* immediately detected a special quality in his work. "It is seldom in Peterhead," it said, "that we are favoured with a sight of really worthy objects of photographic art such as have this week come under our notice. We refer to specimens of calotypes and stereoscopic portraits executed by Mr. Joseph Collier and now on view at his establishment in Queen Street. For clearness in expression of the features, combined with minuteness of detail, they surpass everything we have been accustomed to in this district. Mr. C. is without doubt a rising artist; and such of our readers as wish to secure a first-class portrait at a reasonable charge would do well to pay him a visit. The specimens we have seen are all done on paper, which possesses the great advantage over glass that it can be safely transmitted to friends at a distance and some of the sizes may not only be enclosed in a letter but in a ring, brooch, or locket."

In April, 1862, Collier returned to Fraserburgh, where he was to be in "attendance at the GLASS HOUSE, fitted up for Mr. James Gordon, MID STREET, for ONE WEEK, for the purpose of taking *CARTE DE VISITE* PORTRAITS only, being the fashionable portraits of the Day. Prices - twelve shillings (60p) per dozen. Parties wishing his services will please call early in the week, as he can on no account prolong his stay." Always proud of the standards he was achieving, he invited the public to view specimens he had left with Mr. J. Trail, Bookseller.

D2 below, left, and D3 above : Portraits from Joseph Collier's first studio in Peterhead.

D4 From Joseph Collier's studio at 32, Queen Street.

While he was making his flying visit to Fraserburgh, "a handsome permanent establishment" was being erected for him in Peterhead, at the opposite side of Queen Street from his original glass house in the builder's yard. This glass house was dismantled and re-erected on a platform to accommodate the printing department in his new custom-built, state-of-the-art premises at No. 32-3 Queen Street. When he opened for business, at the beginning of June, 1862, his new studio, "combining every convenience for the practice of his art with the utmost elegance in its apartments", consisted of the operating room, a large apartment covered with glass on the top and sides; the dark room; the finishing room; the silvering room; the frame-making and printing room; and the waiting and show room. It was an establishment which was praised locally as "alike creditable to Mr. Collier and to the town of Peterhead", but which also led to the expectation of "really worthy objects of art at his hands."

D5 *Portrait in a rustic setting by Joseph Collier.*

This expectation was fulfilled and he soon became the leading photographer in the town. In March, 1865, the *British Journal of Photography* reported, "We have never yet received a collection of portraits of greater uniform excellence than those now before us from Mr.Collier. The works of this artist, judging from the specimens under notice, possess more than ordinary merit. They are characterised by the maximum brilliancy capable of being attained by photography; at the same time the half tones are all that could be desired by the most fastidious critic. With three exceptions, all the portraits are vignetted but Mr. Collier introduces the peculiarity of toning down the backgrounds and draperies by a second operation of printing thus leaving the highest lights of the face of a pure white, every other part being in

subservience. We were scarcely prepared to see pictures of this class produced in a northern town of such a matter-of-fact character as Peterhead, which town we congratulate on the possession of an artist capable of producing pictures like the admirable collection now on our editorial table."

D6 *Vignette bust by Collier in 1865.*

D7 *Family group by Collier in 1865.*

28

The imminent publication of a revised edition of the GUIDE TO THE BUCHAN AND FORMARTINE RAILWAY was advertised on 14th April, 1865. A week later, the book was re-advertised under its new title, *The Howes o' Buchan*, to mark the opening of the Fraserburgh section of the railway on 24th April, 1865. William Anderson, editor of the *Sentinel*, wrote the "NOTES, Local and Antiquarian, on the various Places of Interest along the Route (having special reference to the Buchan Section)." A PHOTOGRAPHIC EDITION was to be published for subscribers only. Intended "to show what can be done locally in Photography, in Printing, and in Bookbinding", it was to be an "ELEGANT EDITION, printed on toned paper, with bevelled boards, gilt edges, and embossed back".

This edition of *The Howes o' Buchan* received lavish reviews when it was published containing nine of Collier's photographs. (*D8* below and *D9* to *D16* on pages 30 and 31.) On 25th August, 1865, the *British Journal of Photography* enthused "This is an exceedingly neat little volume, intended, we presume, as a local guide to the traveller, but really, from its handsome exterior of gilt edges and binding, more suited for the drawing-room table than to be stuffed into the pocket of a knapsack-mounted tourist.... The photographs, with which the book is profusely illustrated, are far above the ordinary standard of such works. They are by Mr. Collier of Peterhead, some of whose studies and portraits we have already had occasion to notice with much approbation. Buchan is not famous for its picturesque scenery but Mr. Collier has contrived to pick out the best portions of it and to photograph them in the best way. *Peterhead from the Links* with its fine natural sky, *Pitfour House* with its magnificent Corinthian columns and playing fountains, and the *Village of Strichen* are admirable for softness of tone and clear definition; while

Ravenscraig and the stately square-towered baronial hall of *Cairnbulg Castle* stand out in bold relief and convey an impressive idea of these massive ruins. We congratulate the inhabitants of the "fishing village of Peterugie" on their public spirit in being able to get up and illustrate this handsome volume - the whole work having been executed within the precincts of their own little town."

In the same vein, the *Aberdeen Free Press*, describing Collier as "a man who has the taste and judgment to know what forms a picture in the artist's eye when he sees it", praised him for the "artistic finish and sharpness of outline" of his photographs. *The People's Journal* decided, "The volume is altogether a most tasteful one and would not be out of place on the table of a nobleman. The photographs alone are worth the whole cost of the volume."

By January, 1866, the book was being promoted as "The most suitable NEW YEAR PRESENT from Peterhead. Price Three Shillings and Sixpence (17½p)" and was on sale in Aberdeen and Edinburgh.

At the pinnacle of his profession, acknowledged as the doyen of photographers in Buchan, on 2nd March, 1866, Joseph Collier announced that he had "disposed of his PHOTOGRAPHIC BUSINESS, FITTINGS and Stock of NEGATIVES to Mr. JAMES SHIVAS, who will come into possession on Monday, the 2nd of April next". Collier moved to Inverness and opened his "New Photographic Gallery" at 32, Church Street. He quickly established himself as one of the leading photographers in the north of Scotland but, five years later, emigrated to Colorado, U.S.A., where he soon gained a high reputation for his photographs of the mining communities, the Indians, and the spectacular mountain scenery. (*D17 - D21* on pages 32 and 33 ; courtesy of Malcolm E. Collier.)

D8 Peterhead from the Links.

D11 *Pitfour House. The Mansion of Admiral Ferguson.*

D12 *Ravenscraig from the North.*

D9 *Howe o' Buchan. The Mansion of John Brown, Esq..*

D10 *Inverugie from Mountpleasant.*

D15 *Cairnbulg Castle from the West.*

D16 *Fraserburgh from the South.*

D13 *Strichen House. The Mansion of George Baird, Esq..*

D14 *Strichen from the North.*

D17 *For the first six years after emigrating, Joseph Collier had a studio in Central City, Colorado. With his provisions and equipment unloaded to lighten the wagon, he is shown, above, negotiating difficult terrain during one of his frequent expeditions to photograph the surrounding area.*

D18 *On a hunting trip in eastern Colorado, Joseph Collier is seated third from the right with his rifle across his knees. Inscribed, "Presented to Joseph Collier, Esquire, by a few friends as a token of respect on his leaving for America. Inverness, May 13, 1871", it is now owned by his great grandson, the Chief Executive of the First Federal Bank , which grew from a building society which Joseph Collier helped to found.*

D 21 *Ute Indian. In a letter to George Washington Wilson, in 1874, Collier said that the Utes were on the warpath when he was on one of his photographic trips. After he moved to Denver, in 1877, he took several pictures of Utes in the vicinity of the town.*

D 20 *In the Platte River Canyon. On 29th October, 1879, the Sentinel quoted a report, in the Colorado Tribune, that Collier had won a medal at the Grand Central Industrial Exhibition, "for his railroad scenes and transparencies."*

D19 *Collier was very interested in the life and work of the miners in the communities in the region around Central City. He photographed the first silver bars produced by the Boston and Colorado Smeltery, in Blackhawk, Colorado, in 1873.*

E1 From a painting of Old Port Henry by James Shivas.

JAMES SHIVAS : *PHOTOGRAPHIC ARTIST*

James Shivas was born in March, 1836, in a small, thatched but-and-ben at Scroghill, Hill of Dens, near Stuartfield, which was then a hive of industry with hand-loom weavers. The family moved into the village, where his father worked for a time as a shoemaker, and his boyhood was spent in a house in West Street. The teacher in the small village school which he attended had a sandglass to gauge the time and the only artificial light in use was an "eelie" (oil) lamp with the inside of a rash for a wick. When his schooldays were over, he was sent to Aberdeen to learn tailoring but he found this uncongenial and soon gave it up.

Interviewed when he was ninety years old, Shivas recalled how he was so impressed by the sight of some photographic prints on glass, which were displayed in a shop window in Aberdeen, that he bought a camera and, with a coal cellar in a back street as his first dark room, set about mastering the techniques of the collodion process. He decided to become a professional photographer and, with a small tent as a portable dark room, travelled around Buchan taking photographic portraits. For a short time, he used a temporary "studio" in Narrow Lane, off Broad Street, Peterhead, but soon moved to larger premises. On 2nd October, 1857, he announced his intention of taking photographic portraits, for a few weeks, in Jamaica Street, Peterhead. He displayed specimens of his work in the booksellers' windows and charged a minimum of 2s.6d (12½p) per portrait. In the opinion of one person at least, his entry into the world of professional photography was a technical and artistic success for the editor of the *Peterhead Sentinel* drew his readers' attention to the excellent portraits being produced in Jamaica Street.

Four weeks after this solo venture, Shivas entered into partnership with James Henderson at 41, Broad Street, Peterhead, "for the various branches of Photography, namely SINGLE PORTRAITS, FAMILY GROUPS, RURAL SCENES, STREETS, SHIPS, etc. etc.". They fitted up an elegant waiting room where, to demonstrate their skills in the "various branches", they displayed a great variety of Photographic Specimens. This partnership does not seem to have survived beyond the end of 1857.

On 19th March, 1858, Shivas "respectfully intimated to the inhabitants of Longside and the surrounding district that he intended to take portraits by the collodion process for a period of two weeks at Miss Henry's". He assured potential customers that, "having practised the Art for a considerable time, and possessing a first-rate instrument", he was confident that he could produce likenesses that would give general satisfaction. He was prepared to take "Portraits for Lockets etc." at prices of two shillings (10p) and upwards. Ever conscious of the value of publicising his work, he exhibited specimens of his photographs "with Mr. John Watt, Merchant". Once again, the editor of the *Sentinel* encouraged his readers to patronise the enterprising young photographer. "We would advise those who have not got their portraits taken already to make an early visit," he wrote, "as it is very unlikely that Mr. Shivas will make a long stay or that another such opportunity will soon occur."

In June, 1858, Shivas announced that he would be "taking portraits professionally, by the collodion process, for a short time at the premises belonging to Mr. J. Anderson, Cabinetmaker, Mid Street, Fraserburgh." His confidence in his own ability was growing with experience for he claimed that he would "produce Likenesses which, for truthfulness and durability, will equal any produced by this process." Commenting on this visit, the editor of the *Fraserburgh Advertiser* forecast that Mr. James Shivas was "a young artist, who, by careful application, will no doubt succeed in his profession."

Shivas may have derived some comfort and encouragement from these few words but he was still far from establishing his career as a professional photographer on a secure and permanent foundation. In August, 1859, he was "taking PORTRAITS, GROUPS, VIEWS, etc. on GLASS or PAPER, at No. 40 Foot of Broad Street, Peterhead." By this time, he was also taking stereoscopic portraits and views at prices from one shilling (5p) upwards.

He was listed in the 1861 Census as a photographer living in Main Street, Stuartfield, with his father, who had become a coffee-room keeper. At that time, with no permanent studio of his own, he was still a peripatetic photographer working in improvised "photographic rooms" at various addresses outwith Stuartfield. In September, 1862, for example, he was in Peterhead "taking PORTRAITS at the back of the shop lately occupied by Mr. William Herd, Painter, No. 40 Broad Street, where there is a suitable GLASS HOUSE erected and where Parties may have their Portraits taken in the various styles of the art, on Glass or Paper, in any kind of weather." These "truthful Likenesses" were to cost from sixpence (2½p) upwards. Two months later, he announced that the entrance to his "Operating Rooms" was at 41 Foot of Broad Street.

In May, 1863, he at last achieved some degree of permanence when he "entered on his NEW

PHOTOGRAPHIC ROOMS at 59 Broad Street (above the shop of Mr. Henry, Bookseller)". He occupied these premises, sometimes advertised as the "STUDIO, BROAD STREET, opposite The Inn; Entry by Back Stairs", for the next three years. During that time, he concentrated on taking "PHOTOGRAPHIC PORTRAITS in any of the styles now fashionable; *Carte de Visite*, full length; Vignetted busts; or larger sizes suitable for framing." He also offered to "copy all kinds of pictures - Glass Photographs; Oil Paintings; Engravings etc.".

While portrait photography continued to be his main source of income, he published three *cartes de visite* of Peterhead in April, 1864 at eightpence (3½p) each. The *Sentinel* waxed lyrical. "These little works of art are elegant and truthful representations of our sea-washed burgh," wrote the editor, "and do Mr. Shivas the utmost credit in an artistic point of view. One of the photographs is taken from the top of the rising ground in the Churchyard; another from the face of the said rising ground; and the third from the beach at Salthousehead (*E2* below). The town is shown best, perhaps, in the second named. As elegant little souvenirs of our town, nothing more suitable could be presented to strangers."

E3 Portrait from the studio at 59, Broad Street.

E2 Peterhead from Salthousehead.

Shivas saw the market potential of such souvenirs and, in May, 1865, produced a series of views, including *E4 Bullers of Buchan; Slains Castle* (*E5* on page 37), and *Pitfour House* (on front cover), which he sold at sixpence (2½p) each. The appearance of this series, a fortnight after the announcement about the publication of *The Howes o' Buchan*, with photographic illustrations by Joseph Collier, was timed to remind the public of Peterhead that Shivas was also a scenic photographer. (When a re-print of *The Howes o' Buchan* was issued in 1872, the illustrations - new views of the subjects featured in the first edition - were supplied by Shivas!)

In April, 1866, Shivas announced that "upon taking

E4 The Bullers o' Buchan.

possession of his newly acquired Establishment, 32, Queen Street, the additional facilities he will then have for the prosecution of the business will enable him to produce Pictures which he trusts will meet with public approval. J. SHIVAS having purchased the whole of Mr. COLLIER'S large stock of NEGATIVE PORTRAITS numbering upwards of

5000 and having secured for some time the services of Mr. Collier's printers, parties can have any number of copies supplied them as formerly." His terms for *cartes de visite*, the negatives of which were in stock, were "One dozen Standing or Sitting Posture - six shillings and sixpence (32½p); a half dozen of the same - four shillings (20p); One dozen Vignette Busts - seven shillings and sixpence (37½p); a half dozen of the same - five shillings (25p)." Orders from new negatives cost eight shillings (40p) for one dozen Standing or Sitting Posture and ten shillings (50p) for one dozen Vignette Busts; if the photograph included more than one person, there was an extra charge of two shillings (10p) per dozen prints!

E5 Slains Castle.

E8 Portrait from studio in 32, Queen Street.

E6 Peterhead from the South.

E7 Broad Street, Peterhead.

E9 Portrait from studio in 63, Queen Street.

After Joseph Collier left Peterhead, James Shivas was the leading photographer in the town. By June, 1867, his address was 63, Queen Street, and while achieving the state of the art in portrait photography was was his main aim he also gained a reputation for "the care and due attention to artistic arrangement" characteristic of his outdoor photography. "VIEWS", suitable for framing, were taken to order; in 1867, a picture measuring fifteen by twelve inches cost fifteen shillings (75p) for the first copy and seven shillings and sixpence (37½p) for subsequent copies. He also added to his series of "SMALL VIEWS of local interest" which, "alike creditable to himself and interesting to collectors", cost sixpence (2½p) each.

He produced prints of the ceremony of the unveiling of the statue of Field Marshal Keith on 16th August, 1869 (*E10* below), as well as *cartes de visite* of the statue itself (*E12* on page 39). In July the following year, he was selling views of the "clay biggin", at Linshart near Longside, where the Rev. John Skinner, the author of *Tullochgorum* had lived (*E13* on page 39). These large size prints, costing 2s. (10p) had been taken before extensive alterations were made to the house.

E10 *Unveiling of the statue of Field Marshal Keith, Broad Street, Peterhead, 16th August, 1869. James Francis Edward Keith, often acknowledged as the most distinguished native of the north-east of Scotland, was born in Inverugie Castle on 11th June, 1696, the youngest son of the Earl Marischal. He joined his elder brother in the unsuccessful attempts by the Jacobites, in 1715 and 1719, to restore the Stuart dynasty in place of the Hanoverian George I. Thereafter, he sought his fortune abroad. After a brief period in Spain, and a distinguished career as a soldier and diplomat in Russian employment, he entered the service of Frederick the Great of Prussia. He was created a Field Marshal and Governor of Berlin and played a leading role in the Seven Years' War until he was killed at Hochkirch in August, 1758. He was buried in the village church there but Frederick arranged for his remains to be removed and buried in the Garrison Church in Berlin. A marble statue of Field Marshal Keith was erected, in 1786, in the Wilhelmsplatz, Berlin, where it stood until 1857, when it was moved to the Military Academy and a bronze replica erected in its place.*

E11 A visitor from Peterhead to Berlin learned that, after the original statue of Field Marshal Keith was moved to the Military Academy, a bronze replica, shown above, had replaced it in the Wilhelmsplatz.

E12 On returning home, the visitor persuaded the Town Council to ask for the marble statue. Kaiser Wilhelm I refused this request but gifted a copy of the replica, which still stands near the Town House.

E13 The Rev. John Skinner - author of Tullochgorum, which Robert Burns described as "the best Scotch sang e'er Scotland saw" - was the Episcopalian minister at Longside, Aberdeenshire, for sixty-four years. He lived in this thatched cottage at Linshart, about half a mile (0.8 km) south from the village. The Episcopalian chapel was burned by Hanoverian troops after the defeat of the Jacobites in 1746 and it was declared illegal for more than four people, except members of the same family, to assemble in a house for worship. Skinner overcame the embargo by preaching from a window in his cottage to the congregation gathered outside.

In 1872, he published another series of views. The Sentinel commented, "The points selected are not common to any pictures of the town which have been previously published. Two views from the east pier of the north harbour - one including the inner and the other the outer basin (*E14* below)- make rather pretty pictures. Another view from near the drawbridge shows the south harbour to advantage, embracing a view of the Roundhouse, Harbour Street, and a number of ships in the harbour. We have also three successful instantaneous views, one of the town from the Kirk Shore with the waves breaking on a mixed beach of sand, rocks and pebbles. This photograph includes a capital cloud effect. Another shows a ship being towed out of the harbour (*E15* below), and a third gives a distant view of the *S.S. Labrador* as she steams out of the bay."

E14 The Outer North Harbour.

E15 A tug towing a boat.

He continued to produce views of the area around Peterhead and in August, 1874, readers of the *Sentinel* learned of "several new photographs from the studio of James Shivas, of a specially interesting character; chiefly views of the imposing rocky coast which extends from Murdoch Head to Slains Castle. Mr. Shivas has been careful to select the best points available while he has exercised the utmost care and

skill of his art so as to produce highly finished and pleasing pictures." (*E16* below.)

E16 Cruden Quarries.

Impressed by the quality of the photographs produced by Shivas, the Earl of Erroll commissioned a series of pictures of Slains Castle for presentation to Queen Victoria who, "in a gracious message of acceptance, expressed her great admiration for the views."

Shivas stocked artists' materials in his shop at 46, Queen Street, and, in addition to his renown as a photographer, he established a considerable reputation as a painter in oils; he had canvases hung on six occasions at exhibitions of the Royal Scottish Academy in Edinburgh. (One of his paintings, *E1 Old Port Henry*, is reproduced on page 34.) Well-known artists such as Sir George Reid, President of the Royal Scottish Academy; Sherwood Hunter; John Mitchell; Tennick; and Cairney, were among his personal friends and Fiddes Watt, R.S.A., worked with brush and palette for two years in the Queen Street studio.

Three days after Mrs Andrew Carnegie, wife of the Scottish-American millionaire, had "done the honours", Shivas was selling "PHOTOGRAPHIC VIEWS Of the CEREMONY OF LAYING the FOUNDATION STONE of the FREE LIBRARY". Cabinet size prints cost one shilling (5p) and Large size half a crown (12½p); delivery by post cost twopence (less than 1p) and threepence (between 1p and 1½p) respectively. A photograph of the ceremony of laying the foundation stone of the Library and Museum (*F9*), appears on page 50.

In December, 1894, Shivas advertised a booklet of

Views In And Around Peterhead costing one shilling (5p), or one shilling and one penny (5½p) post free. Five years later, he published *The New Collotype Album of Picturesque Views in and around Peterhead.* By then, a postcard-collecting craze had begun to sweep the country and Shivas seized the opportunity to profit from it. Before publishing his own cards with the imprint *J. Shivas and Son*, he supplied several of the big postcard-producing companies with photographs of Peterhead and district. While doing so, he was not averse to seeing some of his prints, which had already been on sale locally, exposed to a much wider market when reproduced as postcards!

Harbour of Refuge, Peterhead (*E19* on page 42) was reduced to card size from a plate which was named *Convict Prison And Breakwater In Course Of Construction* when it was included in the *New Collotype Album.* A caption combining both titles would have been required to summarise the full archival significance of the photograph. The first part of the prison - on the left centre of the picture - was built in the late 1880s, after the Government decided, in 1886, to use convict labour to build two massive breakwaters to create a Harbour of Refuge in the South Bay, Peterhead. Beyond and to the left of the prison, a Titan crane is shown at work during the construction of the South Breakwater from Salthousehead into the bay. The Admiralty Yard, which was established as an operational base for the Harbour of Refuge project, is shown to the right of the prison. The yard was connected, by a specially built, standard gauge railway, with Stirlinghill, where convicts were employed in quarrying the granite used in the construction of the breakwaters. (*E22* and *E23* on pages 43 and 44.)

Another print in the *New Collotype Album, Old Inverugie,* re-appeared in the *Holmes' Silver City Series* of postcards as *Inverugie Old Castle, Peterhead* (*E20* on page 42); and, after being "printed at our works in Germany", the coloured card *Chapel Street, Peterhead* (*E21* on page 42), was reproduced in the *Artlette-Glazette Series* of *The Milton Post Cards.* from a photograph by Shivas.

The *Grand Old Man* of Peterhead photography died on 10th January, 1930, more than seventy years after he had sold his first collodion prints. Over the years, Shivas produced a veritable photographic archive of Peterhead and District. The prints reproduced in this book are only a small part of his output during the Victorian era

E17 *Portrait from the studio in 46, Queen Street.*

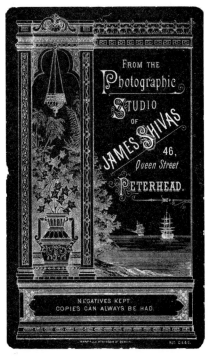

E18 *Reverse of portrait from 46, Queen Street.*

E19 *Harbour of Refuge.*

E20 *Inverugie Old Castle, Peterhead.*

E21 *Chapel Street, Peterhead.*

E22 In September, 1889, this print was entitled "Harbour of Refuge : Termination of Railway and opening out of Quarry." It shows the area from which granite was quarried and transported on the specially constructed railway - officially known as the British State Railway - to the Admiralty Yard, adjoining the convict prison, to be used in the building of the breakwaters for the Harbour of Refuge.

E23 *The steam-powered Titan crane, shown at work during an early stage in the construction of the South Breakwater - probably in 1892 - was custom-built in Bath, in 1891. Tested carrying 62 tons at between three and four (between 5 and 6 kilometres) per hour, it was delivered, in sections, at Peterhead railway station and carted to the Admiralty Yard, where the task of assembling it took thirty men nearly six months.*

PETERHEAD FREE LIBRARY AND ARBUTHNOT MUSEUM

Adam Arbuthnot, a merchant in Peterhead, bequeathed his collection of antiquities, coins, and curios, which he had assembled over a period of some thirty years, to the town of Peterhead in 1850. During his lifetime, the collection, which had acquired a reputation as a private museum, remained in his home in Jamaica Street. In his will, Arbuthnot expressed the wish that his bequest should form the nucleus of a town museum in appropriate accommodation. Soon after his death, the collection, henceforth known as the *Arbuthnot Museum*, was moved to a room in Union Street and later, with the periodic additions to it, to other ad hoc premises in Catto's Hall, Broad Street, and then the Caledonian Hall, Chapel Street.

F1 From a portrait miniature.

In the 1880s, serious consideration was given to the possibility of the Arbuthnot Museum being developed into a *Museum of Science and Art for Peterhead* and being displayed in suitable, permanent accommodation. A Bazaar was held in the Music Hall in the last days of October, 1884, and an Art Exhibition was mounted in the Drill Hall in the following December, in aid of funds for the project. The total amount raised, £1,015. 19s. 8d (£1,015.98)

fell far short of the required sum. As Local Councils were not allowed to levy a rate for Museum purposes and so could not contribute to the project from public funds, it was decided that the *Arbuthnot Museum Fund* should be invested pending consideration of further action.

A request for help was made to Andrew Carnegie, the Scottish-American multi-millionaire. On 11th October, 1889, with the caveat that Peterhead should adopt the Free Libraries Act, he promised to donate £1,000 towards the total cost of acquiring a site and erecting a suitable building.

The Free Libraries Act gave Town Councils the power to levy rates for the provision of free library facilities. It was permissible to devote part of those rates to the upkeep of a Museum, if it was associated with a Library. Adoption of the Free Libraries Act, therefore, would not only guarantee receipt of Carnegie's generous offer but also provide a potential source of revenue to meet the running costs of both a Free Library and the Arbuthnot Museum, if they were accommodated in the same building. After a door-to-door canvas of 1,368 households in the town, 94% were found to be in favour of adopting the Act. Consequently, the Provost was asked to call a public meeting at which the Free Libraries Act was adopted unanimously. Striking while the iron was hot, the Provost then issued a circular appealing for subscriptions in support of the project and over £1,200 was raised. Inclusive of Andrew Carnegie's commitment, the Museum Fund then stood at about £3,400 and so it was decided to acquire a centrally situated feu and proceed with the building of accommodation for a museum and a library.

A site, adjoining the Methodist Church and opposite the Sheriff Court, at the junction of St. Peter Street and Queen Street, was purchased for £1,000 in 1890. (*F2*, *F3*, and *F4* on page 46.) Architects were invited to submit plans for the erection of a purpose-built Library and Museum and, in February, 1891, the design by Duncan McMillan, Aberdeen, was judged to be the best. Contractors were then asked to tender estimates on the basis of McMillan's drawings.

The new building was described as being "in the English Renaissance style in Peterhead granite." The outstanding architectural feature was said to be the seventy-three feet tower "with octagonal dome and minaret. Each corner of the tower has long pilaster lines rising to the main cornice, under the level of the proposed clock, and capped with graceful dome-shape

F2 *Cottage at 21 St. Peter Street on the site of the Library and Museum.*

F3 *A group posed in the cottage garden.*

F4 *Ladies in crinolines in the cottage garden.*

pinnacles. The tower is ingeniously utilised for a part of the main staircase, and for lavatories and a smoking-room. From the handsome entrance hall, which it is proposed to lay with tiles, access is had to the lending library, newsroom, reference library, and recreation room (for chess, draughts etc.)." The staircase, "with steps of granolithic stone," led to the first floor, where the museum and adjoining art gallery, with special roof lighting, were accommodated. Heating was "by the *Perkin's* system of hot water pipes."

F5 From a lithograph in 1891.

All the contracts for the building, with the exception of the special glazing for the roof, were placed with local tradesmen at a total estimated cost of £3056. 18s. 7d (£3056.93). Although, after paying for the site, the Museum Fund was significantly less than the amount required to complete the project, work commenced and Mrs Andrew Carnegie was invited to perform the ceremony of laying the foundation stone.

Saturday, 8th August, 1891, was declared a general holiday in the town and the inhabitants were encouraged to decorate their houses. According to the *Sentinel*, they responded well and "the main thoroughfares were profusely and effectively decked with bunting, flags, streamers, and bannerets." The unique importance of the occasion was emphasised by the fact that the Town Council had engaged professionals, Messrs Shirras & Son, Aberdeen, to supply the main decorations. The Town House and Royal Hotel received special attention but "the crowning achievement in the way of decoration was the triumphal arch in Broad Street at the Town House. It was a threefold arch, composed of evergreens which had been put at the disposal of the Committee with great kindness by Colonel Ferguson

of Pitfour..... The evergreens were pleasantly relieved by flags, shields, and bannerets. Aloft there floated the stars and stripes of the United States, and round the main arch there was emblazoned, in bold letters on each side, the simple greeting - *Welcome.* Altogether, the triumphal arch was most effective, both artistically and spectacularly."

It rained heavily all forenoon but, as one commentator wrote, the townsfolk proved "that enthusiasm in a good cause is weatherproof. By ten o' clock, the streets were thronged. Townsfolk mingled with country visitors, who had arrived in immense numbers by the first train. The railway company had not reckoned upon such an enormous influx of country visitors. In the 10.25 train the passengers were packed like herrings in a barrel. The mail train due at 11.05 had to pass three stations without stopping because it was so full that not another passenger could be taken on, and a special train had to be despatched to bring on the disappointed passengers."

The ceremony of laying the foundation stone was scheduled for noon. This was preceded by a procession of the various trades in "the most spectacular and best arranged parade ever in Peterhead." Representatives of the hammermen, tailors, shoemakers, bakers, weavers, granite workers, slaters, plasterers, masons, joiners, and bone-mill workers assembled in a field on the east side of Queen Street, near the railway station. Having been arranged in order, led by the band of the 3rd Volunteer Battalion Gordon Highlanders, they proceeded by Queen Street, King Street, York Street, Maiden Street, St. Andrew Street, Rose Street, and Broad Street to the Royal Hotel, where the carriages with Mr and Mrs Carnegie and other members of the official party joined the procession behind the Provost and Magistrates, who had been assembled in the Town House. The parade then continued by Chapel Street and Queen Street to the site of the Library.

There was a feeling of regret that "the fishermen - and coopers, curers, and carters and numerous other bodies all dependent on the movements of the fishermen - could not join in the procession. The herring fishing until then had been a comparative failure and they could not risk missing a few crans. If they had joined 1000 strong, with coopers etc. the numbers taking part would have been increased by at least 1500." It is unlikely that, even if the fishermen had decided not to go to sea, the procession would have been boosted by anything approaching 1500. This contemporaneous comment, however, does highlight the extent to which shore-based employment and the consequent economic welfare of Victorian Peterhead were dependent on the herring fishing and its associated trades.

In the absence of the fishermen, nearly six hundred representatives of other trades were obviously very enthusiastic in their efforts to make the parade an unqualified success. They decorated lorries on which, in addition to showing the tools and products of their crafts, they demonstrated some of the skills required in their daily work. As well as carrying national flags and the banners of their trades, they displayed specially made bannerets with a wide variety of mottoes expressing their gratitude to Mr Carnegie whose generosity, they proclaimed, would ensure an improvement in the quality of life in Peterhead.

For example, the hammermen - comprising blacksmiths, plumbers, gas-workers, and, rather incongruously, painters - had transformed a lorry into Vulcan's carriage. One man, impersonating Vulcan, held a thunderbolt and was surrounded by four smiths with forge hammers. Another lorry carried a lighted forge with men making horseshoes. The horses, which were pulling the lorries, were led by pages, "fantastically dressed and carrying javelins." The hammermen displayed the flag of their craft with their own coat of arms, as did the tailors, each of whom wore a green sash and white rosette. They also carried bannerets with mottoes such as *Wealth and kind heart well united are; A Library - the Bible, Shakespeare, Milton, Burns, Scott, Tennyson, and Longfellow; Great thoughts, kind words, and good books are great powers*; and *Free School, Free Press, and Free Library.*

Such typically Victorian sentiments, promoting access to books as the first essential for self-improvement by means of self-help, leading to an all-round improvement in living standards, were echoed by other trades. The shoemakers proclaimed *Scotland waves her bonnet blue to welcome happy days*, and *Welcome Carnegie - May thy generous gift increase our knowledge, our happiness, and our thrift*. The slaters, in their working jackets, with sashes on which the name of their craft was inscribed, carried a flag proclaiming, *We are aye at the top of the ladder*, alongside the town's coat of arms. Another flag had a figure representing art with, on one side, *Vita Sine Industria, Culpa est* and, on the other, *Industria Sine Arte, Inhumanitas est.* Presumably the spectators could translate for themselves! Led by a piper, the joiners and cabinetmakers displayed the Royal Standard, the Scottish Standard, the Stars and Stripes, and the American Eagle. One of their mottoes, *Forget not Carnegie*, was accompanied by a declaration that knowledge, when rightly used, is the greatest power for good, the largest shield and protection against evil that humanity can have. While some of them worked a circular saw, which was mounted on a lorry, others carried specimens of carved wood, with apprentice cabinetmakers showing examples of filigree work.

A lorry manned by employees from James Aiken's bakery carried a hot plate from which newly baked scones and biscuits, with the words *Carnegie* and *Library* on them, were thrown among the spectators. A banner on the next lorry, with men from Keith Rennie's establishment, proclaimed:-
Come see the noble, generous pair,
Carnegie and his lady fair.
The bakers rise in grand array,
And welcome both wi' joy today.

Next in line, were the weavers displaying specimens of fancy worsted wrought at the Kirkburn Mills. A loom was in operation on one lorry while, on another, men were engaged dyeing worsteds in a dipping tank.

The granite workers, the biggest contingent in the parade, carried "a large banner of the Great North of Scotland Polishing Works, being the Grecian pediment supported upon circular columns with the name of the works on top." They displayed examples of their products and advertised the fact that they had won medals at Exhibitions in Edinburgh and Philadelphia. Among other mottoes displayed on their bannerets were *Kind hearts are more than coronets* and *Triumphant will yet be Democracy.*

F6 From a lithograph in 1891.

Led by a piper, the masons displayed their tools and samples of their workmanship. Some demonstrated the cutting and dressing of stones while others were mixing lime. They were followed by about twenty bone-mill workers on a lorry arched over with evergreens. At the rear of the procession were half a dozen butchers "in their white coats, seated in a trap belonging to Mr. Booth, Downiehills" and Lipton's employees with a van and an Irish jaunting car!

After the parade reached the building site and the participants had been suitably positioned among the spectators in the tightly packed streets, the band "played over the *Old Hundredth*, that grand old Scotch tune, and eight lines of the familiar hundredth psalm were sung, led by two companies of the Boys'

Brigade." After the Rev. James Stewart had "offered up an impressive prayer", Provost Smith asked Mrs Carnegie to "lay the corner stone of the building, which had been made possible by her husband's munificence."

Mrs. Carnegie "carried a bottle containing coins, newspapers, etc. to the cavity in the base stone, in which it was deposited. When the hole was filled with sand, she applied the trowel to the mortar beneath, with the band playing *O a' the airts*. The stone was then lowered three times, and Mrs. Carnegie applied the square, the plumb, and the level, in true masonic form, each movement being the signal for renewed cheering. Taking the mallet, she gave the stone three taps and declared it well and truly laid. (*F9* on page 50.) This was followed by pouring in oil, wine, and corn, the last named being contained in a cornucopea beautifully decorated with flowers. The British Ensign was unfurled from the summit of a flagstaff which had been erected near-by, giving evidence to the people who were not close enough to see the ceremony that the stone had been laid." The Provost called for three cheers for Peterhead Free Library and Mrs Carnegie was presented with the trowel, "of silver, chastely engraved, and with an ivory handle", with the inscription *Used by Mrs Carnegie on the occasion of her laying the foundation stone of Peterhead Free Library buildings - 8th August, 1891.* The Provost thanked Mrs. Carnegie, was presented with a

bouquet by his daughter, and after Mr. Carnegie had addressed the crowd and the band had played *Weel may the keel row* and *Will ye no come back again?*, the parade returned to Broad Street by way of St. Peter Street and Errol Street.

The Provost hosted a celebration luncheon in the Music hall and presented Mrs. Carnegie with a vase made of polished Peterhead granite. Mr. Carnegie then spoke at some length. Quoting a verse which his father used to sing,
When Sawnie, Jock, and Janetie,
Are up and gotten lear, (have got learning)
They'll help to gar the boatie row,
And lighten a' our care. -
he extolled the cardinal Scottish virtues of hard work, thrift, a will to succeed, and a commitment, even among the poorest members of the community, to the value of an educated population.

Before he and Mrs. Carnegie left on the 7.10 train for Haddo House, Mr. Carnegic accompanied Provost Smith when the latter declared the Recreation Park officially opened. Eight months previously, during a meeting in Laing's Hotel, a committee had been appointed to consider "the feasibility of taking definite steps for a Recreation Park." In an exhaustive report, the members were "unanimously of the opinion that the field in which the old dung depot is presently situated, from its excellent position and the comparative evenness of the ground, is most

F7 From a lithograph in 1891.

F8 From a lithograph in 1891.

F9 The ceremonial laying of the foundation stone of the Free Library and Arbuthnot Museum. With the Methodist Church, Queen Street, behind it, note the flagpole at the top of which a Union Jack was unfurled when Mrs. Carnegie had finished laying the stone.

suitable for the requirement of a Recreation Park." The Feuars' Managers agreed to grant a lease and, by the time the Provost performed the opening ceremony, an estimated £200 had been spent on levelling and enclosing the area, with another £50 prospective expenditure for a grass mower and a pavilion. (A "Bazaar and Sale of Work in aid of a fund for the Liquidation of the Debt on the Recreation Park and a further Extension of the Facilities for Recreation" was held in the Music Hall on 18th and 19th December, 1891.)

When the euphoria of 8th August, 1891, was long past, there were renewed efforts to raise enough money to ensure that all debts would be paid before the Library and Arbuthnot Museum opened. A special performance of the opera, *Prince Charlie*, composed by Gavin Greig, raised over £12 and the wife of David Scott, editor of the *Sentinel* and a future Librarian, was given the use of an empty shop in Broad Street for a series of weekly sales of flowers which raised £11.14s. (£11.70). On Wednesday, 21st September, 1892, the Earl of Aberdeen opened a bazaar in the partially completed Library building; on the following evening, an entertainment, styled *Twa 'Oors' Fun*, in aid of the funds was given by Messrs J.H.Mennie and A.K.Darg; next day, the bazaar was re-opened by the Earl of Erroll; and, on its final day, Mr. Ferguson of Kinmundy did the honours. The total raised, £756, left the Museum Fund still unable to meet all its commitments.

Four days later, on 28th September, with the comment, "Peterhead has done splendidly", Andrew Carnegie sent a blank cheque to be filled in with a sum sufficient to cover any deficit when the final payments were being made. Since first becoming associated with the project, Carnegie had remained true to one of the principal tenets underlying his multifarious philanthropic activities. As he said after his wife had laid the foundation stone of Peterhead Library and Arbuthnot Museum, "There is no possibility of helping those who do not help themselves, and there is no limit to the good which can be produced by helping those who do. Money had better be thrown into the sea than so bestowed as to encourage the thriftless idler who depends solely on others. One of the prime merits of Free Libraries is that they help no man who does not help himself. They give nothing for nothing; workers, not beggars, receive their bounty."

To celebrate the impending opening of Peterhead Free Library and Arbuthnot Museum, Provost Smith hosted a dinner, for a select party of guests in the Royal Hotel (*F10* on page 52), on the evening of 11th October, 1893. The menu for the sumptuous repast gives some idea of the fare provided on such prestigious occasions :-

SOUPS
Hare Soup   Ox-tail Soup

FISH
Salmon with Cucumber   Fillet of Cod

ENTREES
*Mutton Cutlets   Tomato Sauce
Sweet Breads a la Royal*

JOINTS
*Haunch of Venison   Red Currant Jelly
Corned Beef Dumpling
Roast Beef   Chicken and Tongue
Yorkshire Pudding*

GAME
Pheasant and Partridge

SWEETS
*Gladstone Pudding Salisbury Pudding
Custard Pudding   Tapioca Pudding
Apple Tart
Stewed Apricots Stewed Figs Stewed Pears
Fruit Souffle
Chartreuse and Orange Jellies
Vanilla Creams
Lemon Ice   Cheese*

WINES
*Sherry - Vino de Pasto
Champagne - Heidsieck's Dry Monopole
Claret - Margaux*

WATERS
Sparkling Kola   Champagne Ginger

(It is interesting to note the even-handed "political" content of the menu. The Liberal, William E. Gladstone was then in his fourth term as Prime Minister; the Conservative, Lord Salisbury, had ended his second term as Prime Minister in 1892. In one recipe for *Gladstone Pudding*, the ingredients are listed as 1 cupful of Breadcrumbs, 1 cupful of Flour, 1 Egg, 1½ cupfuls of Suet, ½ teaspoonful of Soda, and 1 lb. Stewed Prunes. Once the stones have been removed from the prunes, the latter are chopped and mixed in buttermilk with the other ingredients before being boiled for 2 hours to provide a typically Victorian pudding.)

After the meal, the Provost and his guests joined an invited audience, in the Recreation Room in the Library, at a *Conversazione* during which they enjoyed a "programme of solo songs, a banjo solo, and the music of a quadrille band"!

At 6 p.m. next day - 12th October, 1893 - the Reading and Recreation Rooms, the Art Gallery, and

ROYAL HOTEL PETERHEAD.

POSTING IN ALL ITS DEPARTMENTS

BUS ATTENDS ALL TRAINS

ROYAL HOTEL

Families, Tourists, and Commercial Gentlemen will find this Hotel replete with every comfort, combined with Moderate Charges.

Commercial Room ; Handsome Coffee & Drawing Rooms ; Private Parlours ; Billiard Room ; Well-lighted Stock Room ; Hot, Cold, & Shower Baths.

Table d'Hote Daily at 2·30 p.m.—2s 6d.
WM. SMITH, Proprietor.

F10 From a lithograph in 1891.

the Museum were opened to the public and it was announced that the Reading Room - where "Aberdeen, Edinburgh, Glasgow, Dundee, and London Daily Papers will be found, as also the Local Newspapers and most of the standard Weekly and Monthly periodicals as issued" - would be open daily from 9 a.m. until 10 p.m. The opening of the Lending and Reference Libraries was "postponed for a few weeks" to allow the Library Committee to raise another £500 for the purchase of books to complete what was considered to be an appropriate stock for these departments - between 7,000 and 8,000 volumes, including those gifted by the Peterhead Reading Society and members of the public.

Two months later, on Wednesday, 13th December, the clock, which had been presented by the Feuars' Managers for installation in the Library tower, was set in motion. Its four dials, which could be illuminated, were pronounced a boon, especially for those who were in need of a reliable time-keeper and were fortunate enough to live in the vicinity!

On 22nd May, 1894, the Library Committee intimated in an advertisement in the *Sentinel*, that "a CATALOGUE of their BOOKS has been prepared and may now be had, Price Sixpence (2½p), on application to the Caretaker. Books will be issued on and after MONDAY, 28th inst., between the hours of 3 and 5, and 6 and 8 P.M. and intending Readers are invited to lodge applications for Readers' Tickets with the Caretaker immediately. The Tickets will be issued, in terms of the Rules, three days after application." The Committee had met its target; there were about 7000 books in the Lending Department and the Reference Department had "several hundred, not a few of which are valuable and useful books of reference." At the same time, *The Times* was added to the selection of newspapers available in the Reading Room. On the first day it was open to the public, the Lending Department issued 66 books - 53 fiction and 13 "general literature"; the first book to be borrowed was *The Palace Beautiful* by Mrs. L. T. Meade. (When the second Catalogue was issued in 1907, this title was still listed, with another fifty books by the same author, in the section headed *Novels and Tales*.)

With all the departments in the Peterhead Free Library and Arbuthnot Museum functioning as planned, the Library Committee were very pleased to announce that the total cost of the whole project had been paid. Andrew Carnegie would have nodded in silent approval!

F11 Peterhead Cycling Club on the Links; 1889.

F12 A Cycle Parade in the Recreation Park during the Diamond Jubilee Celebrations in June, 1897.

F13 A procession in Queen Street during the celebration of Queen Victoria's Diamond Jubilee, 22nd June, 1897.

"OUR GREENLAND FLEET"

Sealing and Whaling

In 1865, *The Howes o' Buchan* - the first photographically illustrated guide-book produced in Buchan - extolled the tourist attractions of Peterhead, "notwithstanding its unmistakable flavour now and again of whale oil and cured herrings". The harbour, from which the first Peterhead whaler had sailed in 1788, was high on the list of attractions for the enquiring visitor. On a walk through the town, "We can show them the boil-yards (if their olfactory organs be not offended therewith and if they are willing to brave a little nasal inconvenience for the sake of acquiring practical scientific knowledge). .... Another scene calculated to interest a stranger may be beheld (but by chance only) from early summer to latest autumn. A sealer or a whaler appears in the bay."

An enquiring visitor, prepared to tolerate the "nasal inconvenience" caused by the boiling of blubber to extract oil, could have acquired "practical scientific knowledge" of the process in any of the three boil-yards on Keith Inch - one on Ship Street and the others on Castle Street. In addition to the familiar sailing ships, some of which were eventually fitted with auxiliary steam engines, a tourist, who chanced to be in the vicinity of the Blubber Jetty at the appropriate time, might have had the bonus of seeing the *Labrador*. Built in Sunderland for the Hudson Bay Company, in 1866, this screw steamer was engaged annually in the Greenland seal fishing, with a captain and crew recruited in Peterhead. On 1st May, 1867, for example, she arrived in Peterhead to discharge blubber to be processed and then sailed for London, on 9th May, to deliver the season's catch of seal skins.

By the end of the nineteenth century, the boil-yards on Castle Street were no longer operating and the other, on Ship Street, was not the profitable enterprise it had once been. With blubber-boiling almost a relic of the past, the offence to the olfactory organs must have been greatly reduced but the harbours and the adjoining area were still redolent of the smells of ongoing maritime activities. This did not prevent, in 1900, a contributor to a new guide-book, *Petri Promontorium or Peterhead And The Howes o' Buchan*, claiming that with "the invigorating air full of the purest ozone fresh from nature's own primeval springs, the visitor must be dull indeed who is not charmed with Peterhead as a health resort"!

When Queen Victoria came to the throne, the town's Greenland fishing industry was experiencing a depression. After local boats turned more to sealing than whaling, there was an immediate improvement, followed by a period of continuous expansion and the port became the main centre in Britain for the Greenland seal and whale fishing; in 1857, the Peterhead-based fleet peaked at thirty-one. From then on, seasonal reports in the columns of the *Sentinel* chronicled the steady reduction in the size of the Greenland Fleet.

In 1860, twenty-three vessels sailed from Peterhead for the Greenland fishing. Apart from the interesting spectacle of a specially chartered tug from Aberdeen towing each of the boats out of the harbour, the main excitement was caused by a crewman jumping

G1 above and G2 above right : From stereoscopic photographs taken in the vicinity of the boilyards and published, in 1860, as Groups of Fishermen.

G3 North Harbour, from a stereograph, in 1859.

overboard from one of the departing whalers. When rescued, he was found to be drunk and was later brought before the magistrates for desertion!

A year later, twenty-one sealing and whaling vessels sailed from the port. Although there were fewer boats than in the halcyon days of the Greenland Fleet, it is obvious from the coverage in the *Sentinel* that their departure was still one of the most significant events in the Peterhead calendar. "The bustle and commotion attendant upon the preparation for the sailing of this fleet, which created no little excitement in our town for some time past, has been brought to a close this week by the departure of the vessels. The harbour, which lately attracted so many by its contents, and was a scene of active and bustling life, is now almost an empty basin of water; and the town, without our "jolly tars", is empty and deserted like. The vanguard of the fleet was led by the *Perseverance* and the *Xanthus*, which sailed on Saturday forenoon with a favourable wind and were out of sight within an hour. The wind veered round next day and caused no little anxiety among the numerous groups who walked down on Sunday afternoon to see the vessels as they lay prepared for the voyage and decorated for "this special occasion", with numerous colours, the figure-heads even being gaily done up with flowers and other ornamental garniture. On Monday, the wind turned favourable and a fine south breeze was blowing; and in the forenoon when the tide was sufficient, the steam tug *Heather Bell*, which had come from Aberdeen for the occasion, commenced operations and towed out successively the following vessels:- *Clara, Mazinthien, Brilliant, Polar Star, Columbia, Dublin, Kate, Elena, Jan Mayen*, and *Sir Colin Campbell*. The back-going tide put a stop to further operations that day but on Tuesday, with the same favourable

gale, the following vessels left in this order:- *Intrepid, Agostina, Active, Queen, Resolution, Windward*, and *Victor*. The *Eliza* went on Wednesday and the *Commerce*, which goes to the Davis Strait, will follow soon after - making in all, twenty-one vessels that sail from our port this year for the Northern Fisheries. On the first two days, large numbers of the inhabitants thronged the quays - some to take farewell of their friends who were leaving, others merely as spectators, but all taking a lively interest in the sight before them. As each vessel passed safely across the bar, she was lustily cheered by the numerous groups at the pierheads, and the gallant tars, gathering for a moment aft, heartily returned their greeting. On Monday, there could not, we think, have been, altogether, less than five thousand spectators; and at one time, as near as we could guess, about three thousand on the various quays at once."

The editor of the *Sentinel* was obviously very conscious of the intense local interest in any news items regarding the welfare and activities of the Greenland Fleet. In the edition of 25th April, 1862, for example, he informed his readers that "A steamer from Greenland (supposed to be the *Narwhal* of Dundee) passed through the Bay yesterday forenoon but landed no report. *If advices come to hand in the course of to-day, we shall issue a supplemental slip.*" (My italics)

In one short news item, on 23rd May, 1862, the *Sentinel* reported two unusual events. Readers were informed that the *Alert* "sailed on Sabbath afternoon for Cumberland Gulf to prosecute the whale fishing." This, of course, transgressed the Sabbatarian code of the fishing community. The report continued, "Mr. Crawford Noble Jr., a mining engineer from Wales, and a small party of navvies went out on board. They constitute a small mining expedition to search for copper ore which is believed to exist on the British side of the Sound in some quantity. A schooner is at present being built by Mr. Francis Robertson, which will be used by the expedition for bringing home their specimens." (The *Alert* appears in *G12* on page 68.)

There were further reductions in the fleet. For example, the two oldest locally-built vessels - the 225-ton *Union*, which had been launched in 1812, and the 273-ton *Commerce*, launched in 1819 - were lost in 1861; in the following year, the oldest boat in the fleet, the 291-ton *Resolution*, built in Whitby in 1803, was lost; and in 1863, two Peterhead-built boats were sold to owners in other ports - the 169-ton *Eliza*, which had been launched in 1844, went to Maryport and the 396-ton *Victor*, launched in 1847, was transferred to Dundee.

Whaling was a very hazardous occupation but the loss of a whaler was not always accompanied by loss of life. If they considered their vessel to be in danger of being crushed by the pack ice, before abandoning ship, members of the crew unloaded items essential for their survival and lived on the ice until rescued. That the personnel involved in the industry had learned to take precautionary measures in anticipation of abnormally extreme conditions is shown in the brief reference in the *Sentinel*, on 14th November, 1862, to the anxiety caused by the lack of information regarding a vessel which was long overdue : "No word of the *Alert* yet and it is feared that she may be frozen in and will be compelled to winter. No anxiety, however, need be manifested about that matter as she had on board, when she left, a double supply of provisions." This stoical attitude was vindicated when, three weeks later, the vessel was reported to have arrived at Cromarty, where she had been forced to take shelter because of bad weather.

The local press reported fatalities from various causes - falling from the crosstrees of the foremast; careless or accidental firing of the "fowling pieces" used when hunting on the pack ice; heart disease while on duty in the crow's nest; exposure on the ice after failing to return to the ship due to disorientation in a blizzard while "on a pleasure excursion to Nayteland"; measles; falling overboard; and, in the case of the six crewmen, who were sent in pursuit of a whale in one of the *Alibi's* boats, being thrown into the water when they went too close to their quarry and "it upset the boat by a stroke of its fin." In the last instance, the *Sentinel* reported that only two of the men belonged to Peterhead, the others being from Aberdeen and Shetland.

By the beginning of 1865, the sealing and whaling fleet was but a shadow of its former self. On 27th January, readers of the *Sentinel* were told, "Active preparations are being made to enable the Greenland Fleet to prosecute their calling in the far North. The *Agostina* and *Sir Colin Campbell* will probably be sent for cryolite, while the others, thirteen in number, will direct their course to the sealing grounds. As some changes have been made since last year, we subjoin the names of the vessels with the masters presently in command:- *Intrepid*, Martin Sen.; *Active*, David Gray; *Jan Mayen*, Martin Jun.; *Columbia*, Mackie; *Xanthus*, Taylor; *Mazinthien*, J. Gray; *Elena*, Maclennan; *Dublin*, Sellar; *Polar Star*, Walker; *Queen*, Brown; *Lord Saltoun*, J. Martin; *Alert*, Murray; *Windward*, W. Sellar. These, along with the *Bullygar* (Milne) and *Clara* (Davidson) wintering in the Cumberland Gulf, constitute the entire Peterhead fleet of Greenland vessels - seventeen in all, none of which will take their departure before 26th proximo." As presumed, the *Agostina* and *Sir Colin Campbell*, were "sent for Cryolite", and so, since two vessels had over-wintered in northern waters, only thirteen boats were scheduled to leave for the sealing and whaling.

G4 Captain Murray in Eskimo dress.

In spite of the reduction in the fleet, the curator of the Arbuthnot Museum realised the value of the whalers as potential donors of exhibits. On 24th February, 1865, the local paper carried the following plea, "The Curator of the Arbuthnot Museum requests SHIPMASTERS and others proceeding to GREENLAND and other parts of the World, that they will not forget the Claims of local Institutions upon any Curiosities which may fall in their way, or of which they may have opportunities of possessing themselves. Such will always be thankfully received." The collection of whaling memorabilia in the Arbuthnot Museum is eloquent testimony to the positive response to such requests. (On 22nd August, 1877, the Sentinel informed its readers that Captain David Gray of the *Eclipse* had donated the skin of a large size Polar bear which, on the instructions of the magistrates, had been stuffed and set up and "is now on exhibition in the museum". At that time, the museum was in the Caledonian Hall in Chapel Street.)

The request for "Curiosities" was well timed for the same edition of the *Sentinel* reported, "The Greenland Fleet is now ready for sea and, weather permitting, will depart for their work on Monday and Tuesday first. Nearly all the vessels have been fitted with Cunningham's Patent Self-Reefing Topsails (No.2)." On 3rd March, readers were informed of the order in which twelve of the boats had sailed, after delays on account of unfavourable weather. (The *Queen* did not sail until 31st March.) In spite of the swingeing reduction in the size of the Greenland Fleet, its departure still caused considerable stir in the town and "The quays and piers were lined with spectators and as each vessel crossed the bar she was greeted with three ringing cheers and heartily wished God-speed!" The *Sentinel* also published the specific times of arrival of each boat in Shetland, from one to four days later. The *Elena* had run aground on Bressay and, even if she could be salvaged, it was reported that she would be unable to sail for Greenland until extensive repairs had been carried out.

As usual, the ships had called at Shetland to top up their water supply and to sign on Shetlanders to complete their crews. By 17th March, most of the ships had left Shetland and those which remained were "detained by the difficulty of making up their proper complement of hands. Wages still ruled very high - £3 to £3.10s. (£3.50) per month and 3s. (15p) per ton being about the current rates. The *Elena*, it was believed, would be got off by the first stream (tide) if proper appliances could be had to float the vessel. Her crew have in part divided themselves among the other ships."

The activities of the Greenland Fleet continued to be a very newsworthy topic. For example, news of the arrival in Lerwick of the steam whaler *Diana* of Hull, on her way home from Greenland, was relayed to Peterhead on 21st April after the captain had reported that all the ships were clean; that is, none of the town's fleet had caught a whale. A week later, readers of the *Sentinel* were informed of the unexpected arrival of the *Windward* in Peterhead. In a verbatim report of an interview with Captain Sellar, they learned that the vessel had left Shetland on 11th March, reached the ice on 17th March, and the crew had spotted seals two days later. Captain Robert Martin, Sen. of the *Intrepid* had succeeded in sawing and blasting a lane through the pack ice in order to reach the seals and "all was apparently going well when, on 21st March, the steamers came up, steamed through Captain Martin's passage, smashed into the pack, and cleaned everything before them, following up the seals and filling up their ships for about a

fortnight, almost within hail of the sailing ships, most of which could not push their way in." The *Windward* "lay beset (trapped in the ice) until 13th April and on getting out again struck the seals and fished for a day or two." The vessel's rudder was seriously damaged in the pack ice and "she bore up on 21st for home" so that it could be repaired. The *Windward* had 2,757 seals and Captain Sellar reported "the other vessels at the fishing to stand pretty much as follows - (the steamers being all but full) *Active* 2,300 seals; *Mazinthien* 1,200; *Lord Saltoun* 1,500; *Xanthus* 5,000; *Columbia* 5,000; *Intrepid* 2,700; *Jan Mayen* 6,500. *Dublin*, *Polar Star*, and *Alert* were not seen." When her rudder was repaired, the *Windward* sailed for the Davis Straits on 4th May, after experiencing "considerable difficulty in procuring a crew."

The Greenland Fleet had very mixed fortunes in 1865. Between 19th May and 1st September, the Sentinel reported the relative success of the vessels as they arrived home. With catches ranging from five tons of seal oil by the *Alert* to a hundred tons of whale and seal oil by the *Jan Mayen* and "three fish and ninety-five tons of oil" by the *Active*, the local assessment of the season was, at best, "Middlin, gey middlin."

Advertisements for the sale of shares in some of the boats provide an illuminating commentary on the state of the industry. Several weeks before the fleet sailed for the 1865 season, shares in the *Dublin*, the *Mazinthien*, the *Xanthus*, and the *Jan Mayen* were offered for sale. (Ownership of the boats was divided into sixty-four shares, some or all of which periodically changed hands.) There appears to have been a lack of the "feel good" factor with a consequent reluctance to invest in the industry. Seven shares in the *Jan Mayen* were advertised at £50 per share; two weeks later, five shares in the same boat were offered at £40 each. Three shares in the "Buchan Seal and Whale Fishing Company, owning the *Xanthus*, with rights to large profits made last voyage" were also exposed for sale. Presumably the seller was willing to surrender the "rights to the large profits" from the previous season's fishing because of serious doubts regarding the profit level in the years ahead. Six weeks later, a different strategy was adopted in an effort to sell shares in the same company. Prospective buyers were assured that, even if the new season's fishing proved unprofitable, they would not be held responsible for any of the costs incurred as "There are ample funds in hand to cover the Expenses of the ensuing Voyage." As it turned out, the *Xanthus* landed about forty tons of oil when she returned on 11th June.

The reluctance of speculators to invest in the industry persisted. The "barque *Alibi* of 328 tons Register with fishing gear, Stores etc.", which had been offered for sale at an upset price of £2,400 in January, 1865, was put on the market in June at an upset price of £2,000. In June, "Five shares in the *Jan Mayen* Whale and Seal Fishing Company, with rights to the Dividend in the current voyage" were offered for sale by Private Bargain. In spite of the encouraging report from Captain Sellar of the *Windward* that the *Jan Mayen* had caught 6500 seals by 21st April, the shares did not attract a buyer and were re-advertised in mid-July.

There were, however, some boat-owners still committed to the industry and it is obvious that they had learned from the incident involving the steamers. Arrangements were made to install a steam engine and propeller in the *Windward* in time for the following season. On 16th February, 1866, the *Sentinel* made a passing reference to this:- "Yesterday, the boiler for the engine of the *Windward* was brought by train. It weighs about thirteen tons. When conveying it to the shore, at the time they were passing Mr. Cormack's, it caught hold of the gas lamp and brought the whole fabric to the ground, smashing both glass and frame work of the same." Once the installation was complete, the *Windward* (*G5* below) sailed, on 5th March, 1866, the first

wooden, Peterhead-built vessel to leave the port with steam up.

Later in the month, the *Sentinel* proudly announced that "the marine engine made for and fitted up in the *Mazinthien* is now quite finished and the vessel, it is expected, will sail this forenoon for the prosecution of the Greenland fishing. This is the first marine engine ever made and fitted up in Peterhead; but for that, none the less successful. On Wednesday night, steam was got up and the engine tested, when it wrought true as clockwork and in every respect proved a perfect success. The government inspector, Mr. Leckie, present on Wednesday night, declared it to be the most successful start of any marine engine he had witnessed. The whole of the work had been executed by the firm of Messrs. Robert Mitchell and Son, Founders, to whom much credit is due. It may be the day is not far distant when we, in common with our more southern brethren, will be turning out our fleet of steamers to prosecute the valued fisheries in the far north." In the following week, readers learned that the vessel's departure had been delayed due to heavy seas and a strong wind. In spite of the new engine, "A tug from Aberdeen was engaged to tow her out beyond the bar... On arriving at the outermost pierhead, *Mazinthien* went bump against the

G5 The Windward. After being sold from Peterhead in 1894, she was involved in the rescue of Fridtjof Nansen, in 1896, and in Robert Peary's early expeditions in his attempt to reach the North Pole.

masonwork, scratching her stern slightly and displacing one or two stones of the pier.... later in the afternoon, *Mazinthien* after tacking about, was seen in the distance with all sail set and under steam, on course for Shetland." The specially strengthened hull had withstood the collision and with the addition of the auxiliary steam engine and "a steam winch, which will be of great service in canting fish etc. when flenching", her owners were obviously hoping that the *Mazinthien* would be more able to meet the competition of the purpose-built steam vessels. (She was completely wrecked in the South Bay in 1883. See page 67.)

There was some further evidence of continuing commitment to the industry. Originally offered for sale, in July, 1865, for £1,600, the *Dublin* was eventually sold for £1,000. In May, 1866, the new owners provisioned the vessel for a voyage, lasting eighteen months, to the Cumberland Gulf. They also fitted a locally made five horse power, steam engine "to warp her through the ice and to be available for flenching, pumping, and sundry other purposes."

In the following year, the *Jan Mayen* had an auxiliary engine fitted and a new steamer, the *Eclipse* (**G6** below), was built by A. Hall and Company in Aberdeen, for members of the leading whaling family in Peterhead, the Grays.

G6 Crewmen on the ice using a manually operated pump to fill the water-tanks on the Eclipse, in 1884.

In spite of these innovations and the subsequent strengthening of the fleet by the addition of the purpose-built steam whalers *Hope* (**G7** on page 61) and *Erik*, the decline continued. The *Sentinel's* vision of "turning out our fleet of steamers to prosecute the valued fisheries in the far north" was not realised. Some of the boats were lost at sea; some were used as trading vessels; and some were sold furth of Peterhead. For example, the 433-ton *Intrepid*, built in Peterhead in 1851, had been transferred to Dundee in December, 1865. The *Dublin*, 328 tons and built in Nova Scotia in 1845, was lost at Cumberland Inlet in November, 1866, and, in the following month, the 266-ton *Kate*, which had been built locally in 1841, was transferred to Aberdeen after being employed in the cryolite trade. In the following year, the *Columbia*, a vessel of 309 tons, built in 1835 in Blackwell, Middlesex, was sold to Dundee owners and the much smaller *Clara*, built in New Brunswick, in 1853, and only 147 tons, was transferred to Aberdeen. Built in Prussia in 1856, the 171-ton *Lord Saltoun* was sold to Norwegian owners in 1870. Two former whalers turned cryolite traders were "sold to a foreigner" : the fourteen-years old, Sunderland-built, 381-ton *Sir Colin Campbell* in 1870, and the thirty-six years old, locally-built, 249-ton *Brilliant*, in May, 1876, a month after going ashore on the northern tip of Jutland.

The Greenland Fleet remained on its downward spiral. The *Polar Star* was transferred to Dundee in 1882. At the end of the 1887 season, newspaper readers were informed, "The *Eclipse* has one whale calculated to yield about twenty-seven tons of oil and something over a ton of whalebone, this being the smallest catch with which she has ever returned from the fishing grounds. The *Erik* has only one small whale, yielding about nine tons of oil, and the *Hope* about five tons and the *Erik* also brings a very fine live Polar bear." The *Eclipse*, with whalebone selling at about £1,700 a ton, was expected to make a small profit but the others were facing considerable losses on the voyage. Predictably, when the *Erik* and the *Hope* were offered for sale later in the year, there were no buyers. Both vessels were eventually sold and, with the departure of the *Windward*, the last of the local whalers, the Peterhead sealing and whaling industry came to an end in 1893.

Cryolite and Petroleum

When the local sealing and whaling industry was in decline and the number of boats engaged in it was being reduced, cryolite was discovered in Greenland. Sometimes known as Greenland Spar, cryolite, or sodium aluminium fluoride, was an early source of aluminium and was also used in the manufacture of soap. According to the *Edinburgh Courant* in June, 1861, Danish vessels, sailing from Leith, and the

G7 Arthur Conan Doyle, the creator of Sherlock Holmes, sailed for a season as surgeon on the Hope, while he was still a medical student at Edinburgh University. In 1882, the Hope was chartered for the rescue of the members of Leigh Smith's expedition after their vessel, the Eira, sank in Franz Josef Land.

G8 The Active, which had a steam engine fitted in 1871, anchored in Bressay Sound.

Peterhead-registered *Gem*, sailing from her home port, pioneered the trade with Cryolite Creek.

From 1852 to 1860, in spite of her lack of weight, the 121-ton *Gem*, which had been built in Peterhead in 1842, was regularly involved in the Greenland fishing but with only limited success. In 1856, the vessel also made a trading voyage to Russia. On 26th September, an advertisement announced her arrival from Archangel with a "Cargo of Tar, Pitch, Spars, Oats, Handspikes, Tree-nails, and Manna-croup which will be sold from ship's side. Apply to the captain on board or to Messrs Robertson Bros. Managers." (Treenails were long wooden pins used in shipbuilding to fasten the planks to the timbers; manna-croup, the Russian name for manna-groats, consisted of grains of manna-grass, an aquatic grass with edible seeds.)

The *Gem* did not sail for the Greenland fishing when the local fleet of sealers and whalers left Peterhead at the end of February, 1861. On 3rd January, 1861, Alex. Simpson purchased eight shares in the boat and he was master when it sailed from Peterhead, at the end of May, "for the Davis Strait". The report of her departure gave no indication of the purpose of the voyage but there was no mention of the vessel in the periodic accounts, published in the *Peterhead Sentinel*, detailing the progress of the local Greenland fishing fleet that year. It seems likely that the *Gem* was bound for the cryolite loading station, the first of at least eight former local whalers which were eventually re-deployed in the lucrative cryolite trade. The *Gem's* employment in this new trade was short-lived for she was sold and transferred to Sunderland in November, 1861.

On 5th August, 1862, the *Sentinel* reported that "the brig *Roman* of Peterhead, Captain Mackie, from Arksathfjord with kryolith (sic)", had called in the bay for orders and that the Danish Vice-Consul in Peterhead had relayed instructions for her to proceed to Harburg. Judging by the brevity of the report, the locally based cryolite trade was still in its infancy and not as newsworthy as it became soon afterwards. Three years later, in March, 1865, readers were informed, "This new trade seems to be improving and extending. The mineral is found at present on the Danish side of the Davis Strait. The *Perseverance* sailed from here on Wednesday for a cargo and the *Agostina* and *Sir Colin Campbell* are being rapidly got ready to fulfil charters in the same trade. We may mention that whalers and doubled vessels are the only bottoms suitable for the cryolite trade as the ships have often to smash through fields of ice before they can arrive at their loading stations. It is fortunate in these days of depression in the whaling interest that another interest has arisen for which our heavy ships are so peculiarly suited."

The 333-ton *Agostina* had been built in Dundee in 1837. From 1840, she was regularly engaged in trading between London and Australian waters carrying emigrants and cargoes as diverse as wool, timber, wheat, salt, bagged sugar, and bark. She was bought by Peterhead owners in 1851 and was used as a whaler and sealer. After a series of very poor seasons at the Greenland fishing, she was transferred to the cryolite trade in 1865 and became a regular member of "our cryolite fleet". In April, 1869, she was involved in an incident which, when reported in the *Sentinel*, provided a graphic illustration of the strength of "our heavy ships". As she was leaving for the Davis Strait, she "unfortunately struck on the outer corner of the north pierhead with such violence as to carry away about twenty-five feet of the coping of the pier besides shaking to a considerable extent the outward portion of the pierhead. The coping stones, upwards of a ton in weight, were thrown down and the damage done is rather considerable. The vessel must have received some injury by the concussion, but as she left the harbour at the time it was presumed she had not suffered any severe damage." The presumption was correct. The *Agostina* was in Philadelphia at the end of June with a cargo of cryolite; sailed from there on 14th July; was back in Philadelphia with another cargo of cyolite on 24th September; and sailed eastward again on 12th October!

As the trade in cryolite expanded, vessels in the Peterhead "cryolite fleet" carried the mineral from Ivigtook (Ivigtut), which became the main loading station in Greenland, to ports in Britain, North America, and Europe.

Built as a sealing barque in Wellington Quay, Northumberland, in 1852, the 184-ton *Perseverance*, was employed regularly in the Greenland fishing until 1860. On 24th January, 1861, the *Sentinel* reported, "This vessel has lately changed hands - having been sold to Mr. John Ewen, Inspector of Poor, by Private Bargain for £1,470. She is, we believe, for the present year at least, to be taken out of the fishery trade." Five weeks later, with Captain Alex. Simpson, formerly of the *Gem*, as master, the *Perseverance* sailed for Newcastle. There is no local record of her whereabouts for some time thereafter but, on 21st August, 1863, it was reported that "The *Perseverance*, Simpson, of this port, arrived at Falmouth on the 18th from Montreal after a passage of 30 days."

In September, 1864, she arrived in Peterhead Bay with a cargo of cryolite, after "a fine passage - ten days from Cape Farewell". Her next trip was not accomplished so smoothly. After leaving Peterhead on 15th March, 1865, she sailed to Granton for a cargo of coal for Ivigtook. "The voyage out was a somewhat stormy one - seventeen days from land to land - during which decks were swept, bulwarks stove, and a boat lost." She returned to Peterhead Bay on 6th June, "having had a fine run of fifteen days with a cargo of cryolite from Ivigtook", and then sailed for Amsterdam to unload. The *Perseverance* returned to Peterhead, in ballast, and sailed for the Davis Strait on 12th July. On 18th September, she was back in Peterhead, windbound, with another cargo of cryolite, which she delivered to Copenhagen and then returned to Peterhead with a cargo of coals from Newcastle on 18th November, 1865.

The *Perseverance* (*G9* below) was employed in the cryolite trade, intermittently at least, for the next four seasons. In addition to carrying the mineral from Ivigtook, she was used to transport stores to the Davis Strait and sometimes returned to Peterhead with blubber. She discharged a cargo of cryolite in Philadelphia, in the second week of May, 1869, her swan song in the trade and returned to the Greenland fishing in 1870; by then, Captain Alex. Simpson had left the *Perseverance* to become master and part-owner of the newly built *Traveller*.

A former whaler turned cryolite trader, the Sunderland-built, 381-ton *Sir Colin Campbell*, was hauled out of Peterhead harbour by a tug from Aberdeen on 28th April, 1865. On 23rd June, she returned to the bay and "lay till Monday, when she received her orders and proceeded to Dantzic" with her cargo of cryolite. Her master reported that another former whaler, the locally-built, 266-ton *Kate* had arrived at the loading station in Ivigtook on the day before the *Sir Colin Campbell* left for home. When the *Kate* returned to Peterhead at the end of July, she was directed to Stettin to unload her cargo of cryolite. The *Kate* reverted to the whaling after being sold to Aberdeen at the end of 1866.

On her arrival home from Dantzic, the *Sir Colin Campbell* was "again charted (sic) for a cargo of cryolite - this time to be discharged at an American port." She sailed for Ivigtook ten days later, after "A new Captain and crew were shipped. Some of the former crew, who caused so much trouble by refusing to proceed, offered their services for the voyage; but the owners very properly declined their assistance." Any superstitious sailors' forebodings, after such an inauspicious start to the voyage, were surely dispelled by the fact that the vessel reached Ivigtook safely, loaded cryolite, arrived in Philadelphia on 22nd November, discharged her cargo, and sailed for home at the end of the month.

Life aboard a cryolite trader was uncomfortable and,

G9 From a painting : the Perseverance among ice.

at times, quite hazardous and so it is no wonder that crewmen occasionally protested actively against their working conditions. Nor is it too surprising to find the *Sentinel* reporting, on 29th March, 1867, "Seamen are at present scarce here. Our cryolite ships are in want of hands and likely to experience some difficulty in securing such." In spite of the pessimism, the cryolite trade increased.

The *Sir Colin Campbell* continued to be chartered for cryolite. She was one of five of "our old Greenland ships" which were reported, in February, 1867, "to be going to the Davis Strait for cargoes of cryolite". The *Sir Colin Campbell* sailed, on 9th April, in ballast, and returned to Peterhead, on 26th June, "with a cargo of nearly 500 tons of creolyte (sic) from the quarries at Ivigtook" and, "having received orders", proceeded to Hamburg to discharge. During the passage from Ivigtook to Peterhead, which had lasted a month, she had been among ice for a whole week on account of strong winds from the south east.

The *Agostina*, which had arrived in Peterhead earlier in the month, had encountered strong winds from the east and had taken three days longer on passage. As is evident from the experiences of all the boats in the cryolite fleet, the time spent on passage varied from season to season, being determined by weather conditions in the Atlantic and the extent and thickness of the ice in the Davis Strait.

Trade with Philadelphia increased and Peterhead vessels called frequently with cryolite. In 1867, for example, the *Brilliant*, a locally-built, former whaling barque, arrived in Philadelphia on 7th March. After discharging her cargo she returned to Peterhead and then sailed for the Davis Strait again at the beginning of April. There was a strong wind from the north-west at the time and the vessel returned two days later, "having carried away her jib-boom." Cryolite ships were obviously given a high priority rating for a new boom was made and sent off to the boat which, to avoid harbour dues, was still anchored in the bay. The boom was fitted before nightfall, enabling the *Brilliant* to resume her voyage with a minimum of delay! She reached Ivigtook safely and loaded cryolite for Europe. After discharging her cargo, she returned from Amsterdam to Peterhead on 6th August; sailed for Ivigtook a week later; and re-appeared in Peterhead Bay, at the end of October, with a cargo of cryolite "after a fine passage of eighteen days". She "received orders" to proceed to Hamburg and eventually returned home, via Rotterdam, on 21st December, 1867.

The *Brilliant* continued in the cryolite trade, sometimes delivering cargoes of coal to the cryolite workings before shipping cryolite to Philadelphia and various European ports. Her outward voyage in 1870 was exceptionally long - forty-six days from the time she left Peterhead to load coal in the Firth of Forth. A year later, when the vessel called in Peterhead Bay for stores, on 4th July, the Captain reported "they were a long time getting through : the ice was greatly spread over the Strait."

The *Brilliant* was removed from the *Peterhead Register* of Shipping on 30th May, 1876, on the authority of a letter from the British Consul in Denmark. Homeward bound, in March, with a cargo of oak, the vessel was frozen up in the Baltic for some time and had returned to port in a leaky condition. On attempting the passage again, she went ashore on the Skaw - the most northerly point in Jutland - and, having been towed off, was "sold to a foreigner".

Ice proved an insurmountable obstacle to another whaler turned cryolite trader in November, 1874, when the *Sentinel* reported, "The *Alibi* arrived on Monday, having failed to reach Ivigtook. About a month since she left Philadelphia bound for Ivigtook and had a quick passage till within a few miles of the entrance to the Gulf where she came in contact with a heavy body of close-packed ice which it was impossible to get through. Seeing it was of no use staying longer, she bore up for home."

The Sunderland-built, 200-ton *Catherine*, was based in Belfast when she was bought, in January, 1874, by Peterhead shipowners for the specific purpose of engaging in the cryolite trade. Her entry in the Peterhead Register of Shipping was closed in September, 1886, three years after she had been purchased by new owners to be employed in the bottlenosed whale fishing.

The vicissitudes of ship-borne trade in the nineteenth century are well illustrated by the career of the Peterhead-owned *Elena*, a 265-ton whaling and sealing barque, which had been built in Great Yarmouth in 1842. After grounding on Bressay while en route for the sealing grounds at the start of the 1865 season, she was eventually salvaged and returned to Peterhead. Subscribers to the *Sentinel* in the first week of June, 1865, learned that "she arrived in port in tow of a tug steamer and manned by Shetlanders who pumped the vessel constantly during the voyage. The damage received on the rocks of Bressay does not seem to be so severe as reported. Meantime she is in the hands of carpenters for repair." The report ended on a distinctively Victorian note. "The Shetlanders who formed the crew of the ship were tall, strong-looking fellows, whose manly and stalwart appearance was subject of general remark to all who came in contact with them. Assuredly the race has not degenerated in Shetland"!

Beginning in April, 1867, the *Sentinel* recounted

further instalments of the continuing saga. "Two years ago, the *Elena* was wrecked at Shetland from which she was brought to Peterhead by the underwriters. She was bought lately by Mr. F. Robertson (shipbuilder), who has now repaired her and put her in sea-going condition. She goes to Sunderland for a cargo of coals after which she will proceed to the Davis Strait for a cargo of creolyte. (sic)" She continued in the cryolite trade thereafter and arrived in Philadelphia on 1st July, 1868. Having discharged her cargo of cryolite, the *Elena* sailed for Ivigtook on 28th July, the intention being that she would deliver another cargo to Philadelphia before returning home. After loading with cryolite, she was "within a few days of the said port (Philadelphia) but was blown away by westerly gales during which she spent most of her canvas." Still laden with the consignment for Philadelphia, she eventually arrived in Peterhead on 24th November.

When the *Elena* subsequently sailed on 11th January, 1869, to deliver the cryolite to Philadelphia, the wind was favourable and it was hoped that "she may have a successful trip". It was not to be. The tale of woe continued. On 3rd February, she was forced to put into Troon "having received damage to her sails and with bulwarks carried away." Five of the crew, who had refused duty some days after she left Peterhead, were tried in Troon and each one was sent to jail for twenty-one days! The *Elena* reached Philadelphia on 14th April; discharged her long-overdue cargo; and sailed for Ivigtook on 22nd April. After two trips to Philadelphia with cargoes of cryolite she returned home at the end of the 1869 season.

The *Elena's* 1870 season was no less eventful. Having received "the necessary repairs", she was the last of the local cryolite fleet to sail for Ivigtook. After a summer in the cryolite trade, the *Elena* returned to Peterhead early in November, after a passage of twenty-three days from Philadelphia with a cargo of petroleum which was destined for a Baltic port. She proceeded to Elsinore to await orders but, while there, dragged her anchors in a strong gale and went ashore on the Swedish coast. The vessel was not holed and, having been towed off, carried on to Stettin and delivered her unusual cargo. The previously ill-fated boat thereby staked a claim to a special niche in mercantile marine history; as far as is known, she is the first British registered sailing ship to be identified by name while in use as an "oil tanker"! (The petroleum came from the recently discovered Pennsylvanian oilfield, one of the owners of which was Andrew Carnegie, who, some twenty years later, made a significant contribution towards the cost of Peterhead Library.) The *Elena's* cargo consisted of illuminating oil which, used mostly for lighting, was shipped in barrels and not in specially fabricated tanks as happened in later years. (By this time, crude oil, seeping from deep seams in coal mines, was being refined in England and, as a result of the work of James "Paraffin" Young, a successful shale-oil industry had been established in Scotland. These products were replacing the increasingly scarcer and less efficient whale oil. It was fitting, therefore, that a former whaler should be among the pioneers in the long distance transport of a new product, which was destined to become a market-leader in replacing whale oil.)

The *Elena* continued her chequered career in the cryolite and petroleum trades. In August, 1873, three of her crew died "of English cholera, as a result of exposure to the cold." Two years later, she delivered 385 tons of cryolite to Philadelphia in July and 400 tons in October; both cargoes were consigned to the Pennsylvania Salt Manufacturing Company. On her homeward voyage, she sailed from Philadelphia, on 2nd November, 1875, with 70,243 gallons (319,331 litres) of refined petroleum for Cork. (At this time, C. Wood, Wholesale and Retail Tinsmith and Oil Merchant, 52, Broad Street, Peterhead, was advertising, "In the Oil Department, a new and highly satisfactory Article has been introduced namely the AMERICAN CRYSTAL OIL, being superior to ordinary Paraffin in freedom from danger, smoke, or smell. Customers requiring it or Paraffin can be supplied with Cans of from One to Six Gallons (4.5461 to 27.2766 litres) or more.")

On 1st April, 1876, the *Elena* left Peterhead for the start of the cryolite season. As usual, the first outward cargo was coal which, in this case, she loaded at Burntisland. At the end of the season, on 26th October, she was reported to have "passed through the Pentland Firth from Philadelphia for Copenhagen." The vessel was "in the news" again when the *Sentinel* reported on 13th December, 1876, that the barque, "which was driven ashore on the coast of Norway, has been got off and safely towed into a Norwegian port." The *Elena* was made seaworthy once more and, during the latter part of her Peterhead-based career, carried cargoes between Amble in Northumberland; the Norwegian ports of Drontheim (Trondheim), Fredrikstad, and Christiania (Oslo); Archangel, Russia; and London, before being sold to a shipowner in Whitstable, Kent, in August, 1880. Three years later, she was beached and broken up there and so the *Elena's* adventurous career came to an inglorious end.

Another of the veteran cryolite traders, the *Agostina*, had also become involved in transporting petroleum. She sailed from Philadelphia with 80,400 gallons (365,506 litres) of refined petroleum for Hamburg on 28th October, 1875, and was employed in the same trade the following year. On 27th December, 1876, the loss of the vessel was reported in a brief statement in the *Shipping Intelligence* column in the *Sentinel* : "*Agostina* of Peterhead, from Philadelphia to Hamburg, oil, was abandoned in a sinking condition on 7th December, lat. 46 N long. 31 W. Captain and crew landed at Queenstown." The fact that all the members of the crew were safe in Cobh (Cork), in southern Ireland, meant that the sinking of an "oil-tanker" in the Atlantic was no more newsworthy than, say, the grounding of a vessel entering the harbour. There was no discussion of the environmental effects; pollution was not mentioned; and there was no demand for rules and regulations to ensure greater safety at sea!

As well as the former whaling and sealing vessels which were re-deployed to carry cryolite, one Peterhead-owned boat was built specially for the trade. The *Traveller* was launched from Francis Robertson's building yard on 7th March, 1868. Described in the *Sentinel* as "a beautifully modelled and well-finished three-masted schooner", the 200-ton vessel was 105 feet (32 metres) long and classed 8 years A1 at Lloyds. Captain Alex. Simpson, formerly of the *Gem* and the *Perseverance*, was to sail as master. He was also one of the owners who, according to the *Sentinel*, had been successfully engaged in the cryolite trade for years. Five weeks after being launched, the *Traveller* sailed on her maiden voyage. Watched by the cognoscenti on the shore, "She made several tacks off our heads and seemed to sail fast and stay well."

This assessment of the vessel's potential proved to be correct. On her maiden voyage, she was the last of the Peterhead fleet to leave for Ivigtook but she was the first to return with a cargo. The *Traveller* soon established a reputation for speed. On one occasion, she took only seven weeks to complete a round trip for cryolite and, as well as occasionally carrying coals on the outward voyage, often made two trips in a season from Ivigtook to European ports such as Rotterdam, Copenhagen, and Harburg. On one voyage from Philadelphia, however, with a cargo of 267 tons of roofing slates for Belfast, she was three weeks overdue when the *Sentinel* relayed the glad tidings that a telegram had been received from Moville, Ireland, announcing her arrival and confirming that all was well.

When the *Traveller* was sold for £500 to an owner in Pentewan, Cornwall, to be used in the clay trade , the *Sentinel* bestowed the ultimate accolade, on 21st January, 1899 : "She was one of the strongest and most seaworthy vessels trading from Peterhead." By then, of course, all "our heavy ships", including her predecessors in the cryolite trade, had left the port.

G10 A peaceful North Harbour; probably in the late 1870s or early 1880s.

Wreck of the *Mazinthien* (*G11* above). In 1878, the *Mazinthien* was sold to Dundee owners who continued to use her as a whaler. Her hull had been overhauled and new rigging fitted prior to her leaving Dundee on Thursday, 15th March, 1883, bound for the Davis Strait. Next day, a very strong north-east gale forced her to seek shelter in what was considered to be the safest anchorage in the South Bay, Peterhead. During the night, the weather worsened. At the height of the gale, after being struck by a gigantic wave, which knocked off the hatches and partially flooded the crew's quarters, she began to drag her anchors. In spite of her engine being used at "half-steam ahead" to keep her bow into the wind, she was driven ashore opposite the toll-house on the south turnpike. When the alarm was raised, the Lifesaving Brigade was called out with the rocket apparatus. By this time, it was extremely difficult to stand against the hurricane. The combined effect of the wind-chill factor and the driving hail caused swelling and intense pain in the hands after fifteen minutes' exposure. It was impossible to see the whaler clearly and so the crew burned tar barrels on the deck to show their position but the Lifesaving Brigade failed, despite numerous attempts, to send a line aboard to enable the breeches buoy to be used. Early on Saturday morning, by which time the vessel was half filled with water and was in danger of breaking up, one of the crew volunteered to warp ashore with a line tied to him. He was overcome by exhaustion when within fifty yards of the beach but was pulled ashore by some of the rescuers. The line which he had taken from the *Mazinthien* was attached to the line for the breeches buoy which was then pulled aboard by the crew, who were all rescued.

The vessel was fully insured but before returning to Dundee, the crew salvaged as much as possible from the wreck and on 17th April, 1883, the *Sentinel* reported, "The hull, equipment, and stores of the *s.s. Mazinthien* were sold by public roup yesterday." The hull was sold, "as it lies on the beach", to Mr. Robert Carnegie for £280 and then the salvaged stores, provisions, spars, etc. "were thereafter sold at Keith Inch and most brought good prices." The *Dundee Courier* later paid tribute to the "indomitable and heroic exertions" of the Peterhead Lifesaving Brigade and *The Scotsman*, in a leading article, claimed that "a more gallant rescue was never made by the storm-warriors of the Goodwin Sands."

G12 *The inner basin of the North Harbour, possibly in the 1880s, with herring boats; inshore fishing boats; and the Alert at the pier on Greenhill, now the site of the fish-market. Peterhead's first Lifeboat House, established in 1865, is the second building from the left. There is a fish-smoking house beyond the Alert's foremast and the entrance to the Junction Canal, joining the North and South Harbours, is at the bottom right.*

"SAUT HERRIN"

Fortunately for the economic wellbeing of the district, when whaling and sealing were in terminal decline, the herring fishing was developing into the staple industry of Peterhead.

The Howes o' Buchan drew the visitor's attention to the bustle of the summer herring fishing. "We can show them, if they come at the proper season, the herring-smoking houses in working order, with their long lines of fish in process of becoming tinged with all the different hues of pale lemon and golden orange. .... Any time in August or September.... from 250 to 300 boats thread their way to the harbour mouth which is most likely blocked up by 20 or 30 boats abreast of each other. .... Morning comes ....

H1 above and *H2* below : *From stereographs, herring curing on the North Quay, in 1859-60. Note the bare feet of some of the workers.*

the piers are crowded with gutters, salters, and all the multifarious sort of workmen and workwomen required for herring curing; work is proceeded with at lightning pace; the catch of the morning is put into its first brine in barrels and, by ten o'clock in the forenoon, scarce a trace of herring is to be seen along the quays." (*H1* and *H2* below, left.)

The port of Peterhead is conveniently located for easy access to an area of the North Sea which was frequented by the main herring stock during the annual spawning migration from the edge of the Norwegian Deep. In spite of this, Peterhead fishermen were, at first, slow to participate in the east coast summer herring fishing. Visitors consulting *The Howes o' Buchan* learned that commercial herring fishing from the port was begun, in 1818, by a few boats owned by a joint stock company which collapsed in 1821. The local herring fishery was then carried on mostly by Boddam-based boats, twenty-one of which were working off Peterhead in 1832. In that year, a cholera epidemic in Wick forced boats, which usually fished from there, to find a base further south. They were refused entry to Fraserburgh but were welcomed in Peterhead. Herring curers from Caithness followed them with sloops laden with salt and barrels and rented designated areas on the quays to set up temporary curing stations in Peterhead, where they were joined by southern curers.

Fishermen and curers must have found the move from Caithness lucrative for they returned to Peterhead in the following years. Its potential for development as one of the main ports for the east coast summer herring fishing was soon acknowledged. Peterhead became the centre for a District, stretching from Newburgh to Rattray, for which a Fishery Board officer was appointed in 1836, the year before Queen Victoria's accession to the throne. In the year of her Silver Jubilee, 1862, about two hundred and fifty boats were fishing from Peterhead. On 18th July, according to the *Sentinel*, their average catch for the previous three days was six crans - a total landing of about fifteen hundred crans for Tuesday, Wednesday, and Thursday; there were no landings on Monday because the boats did not fish on Sunday night.

(*Whitaker's Almanack, 1892*, contained the following entry, which was based on information supplied to Mr. Joseph Whitaker by William L. Taylor, the Peterhead bookseller : "Fish Measure - Herrings are sold by the cran, containing twenty-six and three quarters imperial gallons, on the East Coast of Scotland from Shetland to Berwick, also at Castle Bay and Stornoway; but on the West Coast, Isle of Man, and in Ireland, by the *Mase*, which contains five long hundreds of 123 each." At other times during the nineteenth century, a cran was said to be 35 or 36 gallons; 38 to 39 gallons; 42 gallons; 45 gallons; and, by order of the Fishery Board in 1852, 37½ gallons, i.e. 170.48 litres. A cran came to be four baskets of newly landed, ungutted herrings. Although the weight of the herrings in the baskets, which were used when landing the daily catch, varied from day to day and from boat to boat, a cran was said to weigh 28 stones, i.e. nearly 178 kilogrammes.)

H3 From a stereograph in 1859, herring boats from Montrose, at low tide in the South Harbour.

Sentinel readers on 18th July, 1862, were also informed that "the greater part of last week's catch had been sent to London and other southern markets in a sweet-salted state. The price, eight days old, was 28s.6d (£1.42½) per barrel." In the following year, the fishery was considered to have developed sufficiently to justify the presence of a Fishery Cutter which, as was reported in July and August, 1863, was "in the bay to protect the fishing grounds and to discourage smuggling from French and Dutch luggers." By the end of Queen Victoria's reign, the herring industry was in its hey-day; in the decade between her Golden and Diamond Jubilees, for example, over two million barrels of herrings were cured in the District, mostly in Peterhead, and about seventy-five per cent of the cure was exported.

A branch of the Formartine and Buchan Railway, later taken over by the Great North of Scotland Railway, reached Peterhead in 1862. Three years later, on 30th June, the *Sentinel* reported, "The Harbour extension of the railway is now almost complete and is expected to be ready for inspection, and opening, by the end of the week." The consequent easing of access to markets in the south led to an increase in the volume of herrings despatched "fresh" to domestic markets. In addition, significant quantities were kippered or made into "reds" by prolonged smoking of ungutted herrings which had been soaked in brine for several weeks. The long-term prosperity of the herring fishing industry, however, was dependent on buoyant European markets for pickle-cured herrings.

The export trade in cured herrings was well established by the 1860s. From 1863 to 1867, for example, sixty-five per cent of the average annual cure, which exceeded sixty-one thousand barrels, was exported. Curers aimed at having the daily catch gutted, salted, and packed in barrels as quickly as possible and Commission Agents, representatives of continental buyers, were expected to ensure that vessels for transportation were available as required.

The increasingly complex logistics of the trade are well illustrated by the arrangements made when sixty-one different vessels - four of which made two voyages - carried sixty-five cargoes of cured herrings from Peterhead in 1865. Between mid-July and early November, fifty-two of these shipments went in forty-nine boats, three of which made two voyages, to European harbours such as Stettin, Harburg, Dantzic, Konigsberg, Elsinore, Hamburg, Bremerhaven, and Rotterdam, for consignment inland to the continental consumers upon whom the viability of the herring curing industry depended. The *Onward*, on her maiden voyage within two weeks of being launched by Messrs Stephen and Forbes for a Dublin owner, was among the twelve vessels - one of which made two voyages - which carried the other thirteen shipments to eight Scottish ports. Herring curers were operating in at least seven of these, and so it is highly probable that the Peterhead-cured herrings were eventually shipped to Europe along with herrings cured in the other ports.

Of the sixty-one vessels employed in carrying herrings from Peterhead in 1865, eleven were registered locally. One of them, the *Bannockburn*, whose managing owner was a curer, left for Dantzic on her maiden voyage less than three weeks after the local Artillery Volunteer Band had played *Scots Wha Hae* as she was launched from the building yard of Carnegie and Matthew. The fifty vessels which were not registered locally included nineteen from harbours between Lossiemouth and Leith; sixteen from such diverse locations as Dumfries, Goole, Faversham, Dublin, London, Colchester, Scarborough, Whitstable, and Jersey; and fifteen from thirteen European ports including Bergen, Dantzic, Stettin, Christiana, Christiansand, Hanover, and Stralsund.

Twenty-seven of the vessels, only one of which was

locally-registered, had arrived in Peterhead "in ballast". This meant that they carried no cargo and so earned nothing on their inward passage. In spite of this, some had come from as far afield as Hamburg, Harburg, or Yarmouth; presumably their owners were confident of their earning enough to compensate for the lack of income from the previous voyage. Thirteen of the vessels had shipped a cargo within a week and only three were still moored in the harbour after a fortnight and so it is probable that at least some of these "strangers" had been chartered for specific cargoes before their arrival in Peterhead.

Fourteen vessels had already been loaded with part of their cargoes of cured herrings elsewhere - Boddam, Fraserburgh, Gourdon, Montrose, Rosehearty, Macduff, and Sunderland - and had come to Peterhead to "top up" before proceeding to their various destinations. Most of the boats which had to discharge cargoes in Peterhead before they could take aboard the consignments of cured herrings had arrived with coal from ports such as Granton, Hartlepool, Clackmannan, Sunderland, Dysart, Bo'ness, Wemyss, Leith, Grimsby, and Methil. There were also inward cargoes of staves for making herring barrels from Christiansand, Christiana, and Leith; salt from Runcorn; empty barrels from Stettin; bones from Elsinore; and iron ore in a Dumfries-registered vessel, which had arrived from Montrose and sailed for Findochty with her consignment of herrings.

Carrying capacity was an important feature of any vessel destined for the coasting or Baltic trades. When, for example, the 58-ton *Enterprise* was advertised for sale in January, 1878, potential buyers were informed that she could carry about 105 tons dead weight and, when used to transport cured herrings, shipped approximately 500 barrels. She had, in fact, carried 584 barrels to Dantzic in 1874!

In September, 1874, the *Sentinel* informed its readers, "For the last week there has been a great bustle at the harbours, in the loading of herrings and discharging of coals, bones, and salt. We have had about seventy sail of ships loaded, loading, and waiting to be loaded with herrings; and when half a dozen ships leave, others as many arrive to take their berths." Obviously, as the Peterhead-based herring fishery expanded, the volume of exports multiplied and the activity at the harbour bordered on the frenetic. Contemporaneous records show that, within the month, 80,726 barrels of cured herrings were transported to the continental markets in eighty-two vessels; sixteen of these were registered in Peterhead, forty-four in other ports in the British Isles, and twenty-two in foreign ports. The smallest cargo exported during the month was one of 221 barrels sent by one curer; the largest cargo was one of 2,212 barrels consigned by ten curers.

When necessary, as the following examples show, Commission Agents arranged cargoes by combining consignments from various curers to ensure that they were despatched expeditiously in boats which sailed with loads as near their maximum carrying capacity as possible. When she was built in Montrose for a Peterhead owner, the *Walker* was described in the *Sentinel* as "a fine new schooner of 72 tons" which "by her construction will take a large cargo, will float with little draft of water, and is, in every way, well adapted for the trade for which she is intended". In July, 1874, she carried 702 barrels of herrings, consigned by ten curers, to Stettin; about five weeks later, she sailed for the same port with 700 barrels from six curers. On 17th June, 1874, the *Sentinel* had reported, "Captain William Robertson, Merchant Street, has bought the schooner, *Sarah* of Newport, Wales, a vessel six years old, about 70 tons register, and built of English oak. ... Owing to the big cargo she can take and her draught of water, only 8½ feet (about 2.6 metres), she will make an excellent coaster and Baltic trader." Six weeks after arriving in Peterhead, the *Sarah* sailed for Stettin with 670 barrels of cured herrings, consigned by thirteen different curers; on her next voyage, she left for Dantzic, on 12th September, with 680 barrels from nine curers. The *Jane and Isabella* (**H4** on page 72) sailed for Stettin on 29th July with 921 barrels from nine curers and, on 5th September, left for Königsberg on her second voyage of the season with 920 barrels from six curers. On 30th July, the *Favourite* sailed for Hamburg with 461 barrels from eight curers; on her second voyage to Hamburg, she carried 461½ barrels from three curers. The *Ballindalloch* (**H5** on page 72) left for Dantzic, on 1st August, with 841½ barrels and, on 17th September, with 844 barrels for Stettin; both cargoes were exported by the same curer. On 12th August, the *Nelly* left for Stettin with 651 barrels consigned by six curers and, on 18th September, sailed for the same port with 662 barrels from three curers.

The trade in "saut herrin" must have given, if only temporarily, a polyglot complexion to the usual hameower features of what one reviewer of *The Howes o' Buchan* quaintly called "the fishing village of Peterugie". This transformation was reinforced by the migrant element among the personnel employed by the curers.

Peterhead curers were joined by an annual influx of curers from such widely scattered locations as Banffshire, Fraserburgh, Fife, Leith, and London. Some local curers, including the biggest, James McCombie, acquired their own permanent curing yards (**H7** on page 74) but, for many years, locals as well as incomers set up stations, on plots rented for the season, on the quays or adjacent ground. Prices per square yard (0.8361 square metres) varied with

H4 From a painting: the Jane and Isabella being towed by the tug Blue Bonnet.

H5 The Ballindalloch, built in Garmouth in 1859, was registered in Peterhead until 1879 when she was sold for £203, by public roup in Laing's Hotel (now the Palace Hotel), Peterhead, to an owner in Wales.

the location and amenity of the plot; sites adjacent to the North Harbour were the most expensive.

In 1879, for example, thirteen thousand two hundred and sixty-seven square yards (about eleven thousand and ninety-two square metres) were divided into thirty-eight plots, which were leased by twenty curers at the annual roup. The leading curer in Scotland, James Methuen, whose home base was in Leith, rented four plots near the North Harbour. Measuring a total of one thousand five hundred and twenty-nine square yards (about one thousand two hundred and seventy-eight square metres) they cost £38.4s.6d (£38.22½). The smallest area, a plot of one hundred and forty square yards (about one hundred and seventeen square metres) at Port Henry was leased by a local curer for £2.12s.6d (£2.62½). Two years later, in 1881, the *Sentinel* reported, "Yards were mostly let at 4½d (less than 2p) per square yard, or the same figure as was realised last year. There was a keen competition for several of the stations and as much as 7d (about 3p) per square yard was given for one. Two lots of ground newly made up opposite the old battery (the site of the Artillery Volunteers' guns on Keith Inch) were not let. The total sum realised was £293.19s.3d (£2.97), considerably above that of last year." In 1890, fishcuring stations were "let at the usual price of 4½d (less than 2p) per square yard."

Coopers were the key craftsmen in the industry. Between seasons, they were engaged in making barrels; during the seasons they organised operations in the curing yards. They supervised the labourers, carters, gutters and packers, and were responsible for maintaining the quality of the cure. During the fishing seasons in the mid-1880s, about four hundred coopers were working in Peterhead. Many of them were migrants who had accompanied their permanent employers, curers from outwith the town. At the same time, when approximately two and a half thousand gutters and packers were employed for the summer season, an estimated one thousand of these came from the Highlands. The success of the labour-intensive herring industry was obviously dependent on a workforce, with a significant migrant element, who followed the migrating herrings around the coast at the appropriate seasons. When curing was centred on stations outwith Buchan, local curers, with their coopers, gutters, and packers, became part of this migrant workforce.

H6 *Gutters, in Gerry's Yard, around a farlan - the big, wooden, box-like structure into which the ungutted herrings, sprinkled with rough salt, have been tipped from the horse-drawn box-cart. Working in teams of three - two gutters and a packer - the women were paid according to the number of barrels they filled with tightly packed gutted herrings.*

H7 When this photograph was taken in 1886, probably on a Monday, all the employees in James McCombie's Yard, St. Peter Street, were busy "filling-up" and "pickling". Since boats did not fish on Sundays, there were no landings on Mondays and so the entire workforce was usually employed on the final stages in the preparation of the barrels of cured herrings for sale. After a barrel, packed with newly gutted herrings, had been standing upright for about a week, filling-up with extra gutted and salted herrings took place to make good the sinkage as the original contents settled. About a fortnight later, when most of the salt which had been sprinkled on the herrings had turned to pickle, the process was repeated and a cooper fixed the lid in place. The barrel was then turned on its side and tapped with a small hammer by an experienced employee, who could judge, by the noise produced, if there were any small gaps between the tightly packed herrings. If any were detected, pickle was poured through the bung-hole until the barrel was completely full. (Note the barrels, in the bottom right corner, with funnels in the bung-holes.) Once the bung was driven in again, the barrel was ready for inspection by the Fishery Officer who stamped it with the Crown Brand if he was satisfied that the contents were up to the required standard.

The cosmopolitan character of the industry was also evident in the personnel involved in catching the herrings. The fleet of locally owned boats was augmented for the summer season by "strangers", mostly from ports along the coast from the Moray Firth to the Firth of Forth. In 1879, of seven hundred and sixty-eight boats fishing from Peterhead, there were four hundred and fifty-six "visitors", with over two thousand and seven hundred crewmen.

Large numbers have arrived in town daily since and on Friday a special train, run right through from Oban, brought about one hundred."

The widely scattered origins of the crews engaged in the herring fishing is well illustrated in the contemporary accounts of a strike in July, 1887. The *Fraserburgh Herald* reported, on 17th May, 1887, that twenty-five herrings from the previous season's

H8 Boats from Banff, Kirkcaldy, and Peterhead - with a steam paddle tug beyond - at the entrance (now closed) of the North Harbour.

The cosmopolitan element was increased further by the presence of significant numbers of "Highlandmen". Since the mid-1850s, it had become established practice for men from North West Scotland and the Hebrides to base themselves in temporary lodgings in the town and work in the herring boats as "hired men", crewmen who were neither part-owners of the boat in which they sailed nor owners of any of the fishing gear. In 1880 and 1881, when the number of boats fishing from Peterhead is said to have reached an all-time peak of eight hundred and forty-nine with over five thousand crewmen, some Norwegians also arrived to find similar jobs but they did not return again due to the hostility of the Highlandmen, who regarded them as interlopers and a potential threat to their own future employment. When reporting the "Arrival of Fishermen", the *Sentinel* announced on Wednesday, 5th July, 1882, that "the *S.S. St. Nicholas* called in the South Bay on Thursday evening and sent ashore by means of the *Pride of Scotland* steam-tug about fifty fishermen from the Highlands for the fishing.

cure could be bought in the interior of Germany for twopence (less than 1p) and pointed out that, even if they could get the fish for nothing, the curers could not deliver them to the consumer for that price. Supply and demand were no longer in step and, in such a depressed market, curers were unwilling to risk paying the usual prices - about fourteen shillings (70p) per cran. Prices tumbled to as low as two shillings (10p) per cran in the first week of the new season, when over five hundred boats were operating from Peterhead. On Thursday, 14th July, the boats did not sail for the fishing grounds and over one thousand fishermen attended a rally at Port Henry. Men from Cellardyke, Portnockie, Hopeman, Pittenweem, Nairn, Cockenzie, Boddam, Collieston, Buchanhaven, Port Erroll, Whinnyfold, and Portgordon spoke during a lively meeting. In common with decisions taken in other east coast ports, it was agreed that the fleet would be "tied up" for at least a week. Five days later, the Highlandmen staged their own demonstration. Led by a piper and a standard-bearer, over six hundred marched through the town and assembled at Port Henry Pier. Men from Barra, Stornoway, North Uist, Tongue, Tarbet, Benbecula, Storrhead, and Port Skerra all spoke in support of the strike.

Boats returned to sea on Monday, 25th July, but the *Peterhead Sentinel* later recorded an interesting postscript to the end of an unsatisfactory season. It expressed concern about the "continual exodus of the "stranger" portion of the fishing community from Peterhead, Friday and Saturday seeing several hundreds of "hired men" (Highlanders) leave the town, while large numbers of boats also sailed for home. Owing to the poor fishing, the departure of the Highlanders, it is reported, has been a matter of some anxiety to those with whom they lodged and others to whom they are indebted. Many of the men could be seen on Friday night surreptitiously removing their trunks and bundles from their lodgings and lowering them by means of ropes from upper flats and on Saturday not a few of them frankly and flatly informed their landladies that they had no money this season."

During the discussions about the crisis in the industry, the practice of dumping immature fish on the markets was roundly condemned and several calls were made for the introduction of some method of controlling the quantity and quality of herrings caught, including, if necessary, the designating of a clearly defined closed season.

Put simplistically, the cause of the crisis was the lack of demand for cured herrings at the start of the 1887 season. Stocks from the previous year, when the continental markets had been glutted, were still unsold. In such circumstances, the traditional system of "engagements", under which curers competed to engage boats to fish for them exclusively, all season, for previously agreed payments, was completely inoperable. Instead, the daily catch was sold by auction but the prices reached were ridiculously low and the fishermen went on strike. Less than two weeks after the boats resumed fishing, it was reported that, "Engagements die hard and during the past week there has been a steady continuation of arrangements for the season between fishermen and curers. At Fraserburgh, nearly the whole fleet is engaged and along the coast at minor stations most of the boats have effected terms with the curers for the whole season. At Boddam and Port Erroll, this is the case but not at Peterhead where the bulk is sold by auction." Attempts to introduce sales by auction at Peterhead had been partially successful prior to the strike; in 1887, only one hundred and two boats out of five hundred and sixty were still on engagements. At Boddam, more than half the boats had engaged at fourteen shillings (70p) per cran for August and at twelve shillings (60p) for September; fifteen shillings

(75p) per cran was the contemporary estimate of the price required, assuming an average fishing, to give an acceptable profit for the season.

The engagement system began in 1836 and lasted for most of the Victorian era. Engagements were usually negotiated to begin in the third or fourth week of July because catches prior to then contained too many herrings unsuitable for pickle-curing. The terms of engagement, which were subject to the estimated levels of supply and demand and varied from season to season, usually included a bounty and a guaranteed price per cran for a stipulated quantity of herrings. Eleven shillings (55p) per cran and a bounty of £12 was the average in 1854; in the 1860s it was around eighteen shillings (90p) per cran and a bounty of £35 to £51; and in the 1870s it averaged about £1 per cran with a bounty of £20. Once the agreed number of crans had been caught, the curers, especially in a good season, were in a position to offer much lower prices. If there was a scarcity of herrings, however, curers risked considerable losses. The "settle up", the payment for the season's catch, was not made until fishing stopped and so the curers benefited financially from what was, in effect, an extended loan from the fishermen. In 1874, James McCombie engaged seventy boats and cured eighteen thousand crans of herring; apparently, the same curer engaged over one hundred boats in another season!

In addition to the financial terms of engagement, some curers offered perquisites such as whisky or, something more likely to improve the catching power of the fleet, help in transporting nets which had to be spread out to dry on suitable areas of ground. (*H9* on page 77.) On 13th January, 1875, for example, the *Sentinel* announced, "We understand that several local curers have effected engagements at 19s. (95p) per cran, net ground and cartage ; others at 18s. (90p) per cran for first 100 and 20s. (£1) per cran for second 100, net ground and cartage. For the Lewis fishing, 20s. (£1) per cran and £10 bounty have been obtained." When home-made hemp nets were used, they were protected from the rotting effect of salt water by being "barked" periodically - immersed in a solution of boiling water and the bark of the oak or ash, and then dried in the open air. After the lighter and cheaper, factory-made, cotton nets came into use,they were barked in acacia catechu, the resin of an East Indian tree.

In the 1890s, the engagement system was replaced by daily auction sales in which prices reflected the success or failure of the previous night's fishing and, just as important, the current state of the continental markets. When there was a particularly heavy fishing, prices fell as low as five shillings (25p) per cran but were as high as £2.18s.6d (£2.93) in 1900, for example, when catches were light.

H9 *In the Ives and Wilson Road area, taking up nets which had been spread out to dry after being barked.*

H10 *A tightly packed South Harbour, Peterhead, in the 1880s.*

During the reign of Queen Victoria, the boats in the Peterhead-registered herring fleet were radically altered. In the 1830s, the typical boat cost between £40 and £50. It was undecked, around thirty feet (a little over nine metres) long, and, with a crew of four or five, carried about eighteen home-made hemp nets. After a storm wreaked havoc with the east coast herring fleet in 1848, the Fishery Board conducted a high profile campaign promoting the use of decked boats. Local fishermen were not convinced that decked vessels were suitable for herring fishing. Several bigger boats with minimal facilities for the crew - a small cabin with a couple of bunks and a stove - were built in the 1850s and the port's first decked herring boat, the *Fisherman's Friend*, came into service in 1858. It was not until ten years later, however, that there is much evidence that a significant number of local fishermen had been persuaded to adopt decked vessels. The *Sentinel* reported, "Boatbuilders are at present very busy. Messrs Stephen and Forbes have orders on hand for 30 herring boats - the orders of the others in the trade must be considerable - all of which will have to be completed before the commencement of the fishing." Four months later, readers were informed, "We observe that several decked fishing boats of large dimensions, elegant model, and first class workmanship have been built by Messrs Stephen and Forbes for fishermen in the locality. These boats are a great improvement on the old style and will, we believe, give every satisfaction."

The adoption of the improved style of boat continued. In March, 1883, for example, in anticipation of the ensuing fishing season, Stephen and Forbes were reported to "have already launched fourteen herring fishing boats while two others are almost ready." At the same time, "A new development in the direction of improved appliances for the prosecution of the herring and other fisheries was inaugurated in Peterhead by the launch of the ketch *Annie* of Peterhead, built for Mr. Cummin Summers, fisherman of Peterhead." The 55-ton boat, launched by Stephen and Forbes, measured 70 feet (21.3 metres) overall and 18½ feet (5.6 metres) broad, with a hold 9 feet (2.7 metres) deep. The press reported the innovative features in detail. "The new craft is fitted up with fore and aft cabins, the former with beds for eight and the aft with beds for five men. An apartment forward has been fitted up for holding nets while at the opposite end of the hold is a similar division for the bush rope, or line to which nets and fishing lines are attached. On deck, is a patent three horse power capstan for net-hauling purposes. She is carvel square built throughout and has a frame constructed of similar strength to that of an ordinary

sailing ship of similar tonnage. It is intended that she engage in the Lewis and Shetland herring fishing, then the autumn fishing on the east coast. She will carry materials for the curing of herring on board and her crew will comprise a number of boys for gutting and packing. She will always be provisioned for remaining at least a week at sea and when not engaged at herring fishing will be engaged at deep sea fishing and trawling." The report ended by informing readers that Carnegie and Matthew had a smack similar to the *Annie* on the stocks. This type of multi-purpose embryonic "factory ship" was very uncommon and the herring fishermen of Peterhead continued to use the conventional drifter.

The catching power of the fleet was increased several times over when hemp nets were replaced by the lighter cotton variety and, with bigger and better boats, fishermen ventured further offshore in search of better quality herrings. By the end of the 1870s, stoutly timbered, carvel-built boats, fitted with a winch, and carrying fifty nets were, with six in a crew, capable of fishing as much as sixty miles offshore if required. As the century drew to a close, there was a gradual decrease in the number of Peterhead-based herring boats. By 1896, it was around three hundred fewer than it had been fifteen years earlier. The catching power did not decline, however, thanks to the improvements in boats and equipment, the latest of which was the installation of steam-powered capstans from 1896 onwards.

Although the *Sentinel* had reported, as early as July, 1868, that a herring drifter - built by Messrs Hall, Aberdeen, with a nine horse power engine and capable of steaming at six to seven knots an hour - was "on view" in Peterhead harbour, it was not until 1900 that the first Peterhead-owned steam drifters began fishing from the port. In the same year, two steel, purpose-built drifters were launched for a local company which had been formed to prosecute the herring fishing with steam-powered vessels. These heralds of a new era in the history of herring fishing cost more than £3000 each, nearly four times as much as seventy-feet long, wooden, sailing drifters built just two years previously.

In spite of the vast increase in the cost of fitting out a vessel ready for sea, the long-established tradition of members of the crew being part-owners of the boats continued. In the years following the death of Queen Victoria, with the help of investments by, among others, coal merchants, ship chandlers, fish salesmen, and curers, the fleet of sailing-boats was rapidly replaced by a fleet of modern steam drifters whose managing owners were often fishing skippers.

H11 *Built at Neath Abbey in 1876-77, the paddle steamer, Flying Scud, was bought for £1,300, in 1895, to act as the Peterhead Harbour Tug.*

PETERHEAD-BUILT

The author of *The Howes o' Buchan* highlighted another burgeoning industry as a tourist attraction in Victorian Peterhead. "We can show them," he wrote, " the shipbuilding yards - neither few in number nor insignificant - which can turn out ships able to compete for the belt of the ocean with the best of the Aberdeen clippers."

Aware of the port's reputation as a base for the Greenland fishing, a visitor on a conducted tour of the shipbuilding yards in 1865, might have been surprised to find no whaling or sealing vessels on the stocks. A knowledgeable carpenter could have told the tourist that the 321-ton *Windward*, the last of "our heavy ships" to be built in the port, had been launched in 1860 by Messrs Stephen and Forbes. He could also have added that at least fourteen whalers or sealers had left the ways in local yards in the twenty-one years before then; that is, a total of fifteen vessels as identified by * in the table on page 81. The visitor might have been equally surprised to learn that, as well as these additions to the Greenland fleet and fishing boats of various sizes, the yards had been busy turning out merchant vessels capable of "holding their own" on every trade route worldwide.

The most productive builders were Stephen and Forbes on Bridge Street; Carnegie and Matthew on the north side of Fish Lane on the Seagate, or North Shore; and, also on the North Shore, Lunnan and Robertson - later Francis Robertson - on the north side of Brook Lane (*J1* below).

Arrangements for launching vessels on the North Shore were complicated, in 1865, when the railway was extended from the town station, via Roanheads, along the Seagate, to the South Harbour. Announcing an "Improvement on the North Shore", the *Sentinel*, on 29th March, 1867, reported that there was "now a fine clean promenade extending from Union Street to the building yard at Brook Lane" and "The ugly protruding dyke which ran along the shore in front of the building yard of Carnegie and Matthew is now removed and carried out in a line with the railway paling, thus adding some twelve or fourteen feet to the breadth of the street running from the foot of Fish Lane to that of Brook Lane." While these alterations may have been aesthetically pleasing and convenient for traffic on the Seagate, they did nothing to remove the problems posed by the railway running between the yards and the water into which boats had to be launched. These difficulties remained until the harbour railway extension was shortened and sidings built between Port Henry and Roanheads, in 1896, by which time the heyday of the Peterhead ship-building industry had long since passed.

The table, which is not presented as definitive, has been compiled from contemporaneous sources - *Registers of Shipping; Registration of Transactions relating to ships registered under 8th and 9th Victoria, Cap 89 for 1845-1899; Lloyd's Registers of Shipping;* and copies of the *Sentinel* from 1857 onwards. The vessels are not directly comparable in size because some of the tonnages were given, at the time of launching, in Builder's Measure, while others were in New Measure; and some were re-measured after being re-classified subsequent to alterations.

J1 From a painting: the North Shore, with, on the extreme right, flags flying above the stern of the Jan Mayen, which was being prepared for launching.

Year	Name	Tonnage	Builder
1837	*Francis*	148	
	Union	56	
1838	*Copy*	112	
1839	*Enterprise*	22	Scott and Stevenson
	*Mary Ann Henderson	132	Scott and Stevenson
1840	**Brilliant*	249	
	Jane Geary	228	
	*Reliance	242	
1841	**Kate*	266	Scott and Stevenson
1842	**Gem*	121	
1843	*Margaret and Jane*	29	
	Rosebud	103	
1844	**Eliza*	169	Scott and Stevenson
	*Queen	369	Alexander Geddes
1845	*Hero*	43	Lunnan and Robertson
	*Xanthus	217	Alexander Geddes
1846	*Haidee*	80	
	Lima	349	
1847	*Alert*	215	
	Coromandel	393	Lunnan and Robertson
	Jenny Lind	93	Lunnan and Robertson
	Lord Haddo	340	
	*Victor	396	John Taylor and Son
1848	*Balmoral*	345	Alexander Geddes
	Elizabeth	22	Alexander Ingram
	Industry	96	Lunnan and Robertson
	Ochtertyre	222	
	Vivid	101	Lunnan and Robertson
1849	*Annie*	119	Lunnan and Robertson
	Dreadnaught	330	
	Janet	18	Scott and Stevenson
	Rapid	107	Lunnan and Robertson
1850	*Breeze*	136	
	Hamilla Mitchell	540	
1851	*Active*	78	Scott and Stevenson
	Elizabeth	125	
	*Intrepid	434	Francis Robertson
1852	**Active*	348	Francis Robertson
	May Queen	75	John Taylor and Son
1853	**Alert*	116	Francis Robertson
	Ellon Castle	348	
1854	*Governess*	244	
	Leonidas	320	Francis Robertson
1855	*Sprite*	90	
1856	*Arrow*	95	Francis Robertson
	Ocean	92	
1857	**Polar Star*	216	Stephen and Forbes
	Sentinel	31	Stephen and Forbes
1858	*Lightning*	79	Stephen and Forbes
	Onward	84	Francis Robertson?
	Yarrow (Yarra)	185	Francis Robertson
1859	**Jan Mayen*	337	Francis Robertson
	Swift	30	Carnegie and Matthew
1860	*Hugh Miller*	102	Carnegie and Matthew
	Volunteer	52	Stephen and Forbes
	*Windward	321	Stephen and Forbes
	Vesper	100	Stephen and Forbes

Year	Name	Tonnage	Builder
1861	*Vistula*	87	Stephen and Forbes
	Wave	80	Francis Robertson
	Jane and Isabella	90	Carnegie and Matthew
1862	*Bullygar*	87	Francis Robertson
	Charlotte Andrews	356	Francis Robertson
	David Ewan	115	Stephen and Forbes
	Hawk	45	Carnegie and Matthew
	Mary-Anne	18	Stephen and Forbes
	Teaser	67	Stephen and Forbes
1863	*Charm*	39	Stephen and Forbes
	Princess of Wales	157	Stephen and Forbes
	Prospector	236	Francis Robertson
1864	*Helen* **		
	Inverugie	233	Stephen and Forbes
	Marshal Keith	130	Carnegie and Matthew
	Southland	270	Francis Robertson
1865	*Ayr*	287	Francis Robertson
	Bannockburn	100	Carnegie and Matthew
	Conoid	168	Carnegie and Matthew
	Conquest	41	Stephen and Forbes
	Onward	56	Stephen and Forbes
	Star of Hope	261	Stephen and Forbes
1866	*Delight*	104	Francis Robertson
	Milina	95	Francis Robertson
	Pitfour	267	Stephen and Forbes
	Star of Scotia	92	Carnegie and Matthew
	Stinchar	393	Francis Robertson
	Wallace	167	Carnegie and Matthew
1867	*Annie*	124	Francis Robertson
	Eclipse	67	Stephen and Forbes
	Flower o' Buchan	99	Carnegie and Matthew
	Garron	190	Stephen and Forbes
	Inverary	285	Francis Robertson
1868	*Craigewan*	203	Stephen and Forbes
	Elderslie	215	Carnegie and Matthew
	Floral Star	250	Stephen and Forbes
	Rattray	284	Carnegie and Matthew
	Sweet Home	30	James Florence
1868	*Traveller*	200	Francis Robertson
1869	*Estelle*	208	Messrs Birnie
	Lord of the Isles	328	Stephen and Forbes
	Rosedud	202	Carnegie and Matthew
	Velocipede	32	Carnegie and Matthew
1870	*Albion*	60	Carnegie and Matthew
	Ariel	86	Stephen and Forbes
	Enterprise	58	Carnegie and Matthew
	Nelly	68	Stephen and Forbes
	Vixen	189	Stephen and Forbes
1871	*Jessie McDonald*	300	Stephen and Forbes
	Mermaid	72	Carnegie and Matthew
1872	*Olive Branch*	191	Carnegie and Matthew
1873	*Countess of Erroll*	180	Stephen and Forbes
	Helen Hutchison	81	Carnegie and Matthew
	Paragon	105	Carnegie and Matthew
	Tullochgorum	186	Stephen and Forbes
	Viking	108	Stephen and Forbes.
1874	*Mary Ann*	86	Carnegie and Matthew

Year	Name	Tonnage	Builder
1875	*Express*	99	Carnegie and Matthew
	Lochiel	228	Stephen and Forbes
	Wandering Minstrel	362	Stephen and Forbes
1876	*Ebenezer*	340	Stephen and Forbes
	Forward	113	Stephen and Forbes
	Robert	117	Carnegie and Matthew
	Rosebud	352	Carnegie and Matthew
1877	*Baltic*	110	Carnegie and Matthew
	Beaconsfield	75	Carnegie and Matthew
	Resolute	127	Stephen and Forbes
1878	*Lady Cecilia Hay*	75	Stephen and Forbes
	Maggie	118	Stephen and Forbes
	Minnie	108	Carnegie and Matthew
	Promise		James Florence
1879	*Paragon*	120	Stephen and Forbes
1880	*Eira*	260	Stephen and Forbes
	Sovereign	103	Carnegie and Matthew
1881	*Aldana Castle*	90	Carnegie and Matthew
	Victory		Wilson and Daniel
1882	*C.S.Parnell*	74	Stephen and Forbes
1885	*Welcome Home*	63	Stephen and Forbes

N.B. ** The *Helen* was built as a fishing vessel but was used latterly as a Leith trader.

J2 From a painting: the Princess of Wales.

"The Tonnage of Our Port"

During the first twenty years of Queen Victoria's reign, before the weekly editions of the *Sentinel* kept its readers informed of the world-wide activities of vessels built in Peterhead, entries in *Lloyd's Registers of Shipping* indicated the far-flung charters undertaken by several of these boats. Some of these were registered locally but others had been sold to ports such as Aberdeen, Dundee, Glasgow, and London. In 1844, for example, the *Copy* was reported to be on passage from London to Africa. Nine years later, the *Annie* and the *Lord Haddo* were bound for the Cape of Good Hope; the *Balmoral* was en route for Ceylon; the *Coromandel* was on a voyage from London to Montreal; the *Dreadnaught* and the *Lima* were sailing from London for ports in Australia; the *Hamilla Mitchell* was chartered for Hong Kong; and the *Industry* was on passage from Aberdeen to the Mediterranean. In 1857, the *Ellon Castle* was reported to be bound from London to Mauritius; the *Hamilla Mitchell* was on passage from London to China; the *Lord Haddo* was chartered from the Clyde to the West Indies; and the *Ochtertyre* was en route from Liverpool to Algoa Bay.

The *Sentinel* made a point of describing, often in considerable detail, the ceremonial launching of locally built boats. Some of these were subsequently sold furth of the town and, unless they "hit the headlines" for a particularly newsworthy reason, were seldom featured in the columns of the *Sentinel* thereafter. Readers were kept informed, however, of the activities of the Peterhead registered merchant fleet which was frequently referred to as "the tonnage of our port". The tonnage registered in the town included vessels which, built elsewhere, had been bought by local shipowners; the boats featured in this chapter were all launched from local yards. In addition to publishing data regarding the movement of vessels in and out of the harbours and the bay, the *Sentinel* copied relevant items from the foreign press; relayed messages received by telegraph; and also reported sightings - by shore-based observers or by crews of other vessels - of Peterhead boats on passage.

As the following examples show, a significant number of the vessels comprising "the tonnage of our port" ranged far and wide along the inter-continental trade routes in a constant effort to be continuously chartered with suitable freight. Details of the voyages, including the times spent on passage, not only delineate the commonly frequented areas and identify the main ports of call, but also help to illustrate the living and working conditions endured by the Victorian merchant seamen.

Stephen and Forbes launched the 157-ton *Princess of Wales* (*J2* on page 83) in August, 1863. Built for

local owners and designed for the Mediterranean trade, the three-masted schooner was described as "a fine piece of marine architecture, classed A1 for 7 years, being copper-bottomed and provided with all the latest improvements in gear." On 11th December, 1863, the *Sentinel* was pleased to deny a rumour, prevalent in the town, that the *Princess of Wales* had been lost. The vessel had sailed from Peterhead for Newcastle on 9th September, 1863, and then proceeded to Pillau (Baltisk near Kaliningrad in Russia). On the return voyage from Pillau to Leith, she struck a sandbank but, after discharging part of her cargo, had floated off and reached Copenhagen safely. The more superstitious members of the seafaring fraternity might have claimed that they knew some mishap was bound to befall the vessel early in her career; her launch had to be postponed for a day after the first attempt to move her down the ways had ended in failure! The boat's apparent bad luck continued while on passage to Dantzic from Messina, Sicily. She had to be towed into Elsinore, Denmark, on 10th March, 1865, and did not reach Dantzic until five weeks later.

Nearly nine years after leaving the stocks in the builders' yard, the *Princess of Wales* was completely overhauled before being re-classed at Lloyd's. The local cognoscenti pronounced, "She still stands the smartest little vessel out of the port and there can be little doubt of her continued success." Their judgment was completely vindicated within the next eight months. She reached Pillau on 21st April, 1872, and was reported, on 21st May, to have passed Elsinore on her way from Königsberg (Kaliningrad) to Dundee, where she arrived on 1st June. By 17th July, she had passed Gibraltar en route from Granton for Zante (later known as Zakinthos), an island in the Ionian Sea. After reaching Zante, on 6th August, she called at Cephalonia (Kefallinia), another of the Ionian islands, and then sailed for Montreal, Canada, where she arrived on 29th October.

During the passage home, the *Princess of Wales* experienced "continual heavy gales, attended with a very high cross sea, showers of hail and snow, and much lightning." Quoting from a letter, posted by the Master, Captain Ewan, after the vessel's safe arrival in Waterford, Ireland, the *Sentinel* informed its readers, on 11th December, 1872, that he " had never seen weather like it before in the North Atlantic and hardly thought to get through it. When in lat 47 N and long 78 W, they came upon the *Pride of the Ocean*, of 1,362 tons, belonging to South Shields, with her boats all gone, her decks completely swept, waterlogged and breaking up fast, and the crew, 24 in number, along with the captain's wife, in the three tops. The *Princess of Wales* lay by them for three days and nights, sailing round and round them but unable, because of the tremendous sea, to do anything for them. On the fourth day, however, it moderated somewhat and they were able to rescue the crew and captain's wife by means of the small boat." In conclusion, Captain Ewan said that no ship or barque could have gone round the disabled ship as the *Princess of Wales* had done. Ten weeks later, on 19th February, 1873, the *Sentinel* proudly announced that the Board of Trade had "awarded to Captain Ewan an Aneroid barometer as a mark of appreciation of the services rendered by him to the crew of the *Pride of the Ocean.*"

By then, the *Princess of Wales* was en route from Cardiff to Palermo. She then sailed for New York, called at Boston, and had returned to Lisbon on 6th June. During the next three years, her ports of call included Leith; Patras (Patrai) in Greece; Falmouth; Truro; Zante; St. Petersburg; Grangemouth; Liverpool; Catanzaro in Southern Italy; St. Nazaire; Nantes; Sonderborg in Denmark; and Pillau. The *Princess of Wales* sailed for Belfast, with a load of tares from Pillau, on 15th December, 1876. On Christmas Eve, she was abandoned in a sinking condition and foundered about seventy miles North East of Kinnaird Head. Fortunately, the crew were picked up by a Norwegian vessel and landed safely at Christiansand.

On 24th June, 1864, the *Sentinel* reported that the newly built *Inverugie* had accommodation for fourteen passengers and "the Peterhead coat of arms upon her skylight, which also is after a very chaste design". Intended for employment on the coast of South Africa, "for which trade she is admirably adapted", she left Peterhead in the first week of August, 1864, bound for London, whence she was scheduled to sail for Algoa Bay, Cape Province. It seems, however, that her owners had decided not to adhere to their original business plan. The *Inverugie* left Algoa Bay on 22nd January, 1865; reached Mauritius twenty days later; and sailed for Melbourne, Australia, on 17th March. She had justified "the high expectations which were entertained of her sailing powers, having made the voyage from Mauritius in thirty-six days, after a very rough passage. Several of the other ships, which left along with the *Inverugie*, had their decks completely swept. The first arrival of these vessels was seven days after the Inverugie and the latest fourteen days." When the *Sentinel* proudly reported this achievement, it also informed its readers that the vessel was scheduled to leave Melbourne for Valparaiso, Chile, on 26th May.

Having spent most of her first year in service in waters outwith her intended sphere of operations, the *Inverugie* continued to be employed in inter-continental trade. Early in January, 1868, for example, she sailed from Liverpool for Rio Grande do Norte, Brazil, and, as reported locally, "on 12th February, while taking the river, during a strong breeze, blowing dead on to the shore, she was grounded on a bank in the river. Next tide she filled with water. All hands are safe and part of the cargo saved but in a damaged state." Two months later, the owners were informed that the *Inverugie* had been towed off the strand and was loading sugar and cotton for Liverpool. By 27th May, 1868, the *Inverugie* was back in Peterhead with a cargo of salt from Runcorn and then, at the end of July, sailed for Newcastle, in ballast.

As long as she remained on the *Peterhead Register*, in addition to indicating her immediate destination, entries in her log must often have added, in the parlance of the day, "and thence as required to any other port or place, as employment may be found." Readers of the *Sentinel* were kept informed of many of the vessel's charters. On 9th April, 1872, for example, she was in Palermo, Sicily, and then called at Cagliari, Sardinia, before sailing via Falmouth to Antwerp, Belgium, where she docked on 21st June, 1872. By 20th November, she had arrived in Liverpool from Girgenti (Agrigento), Sicily, and was reported, on 5th February, 1873, to have left Liverpool for Rio de Janeiro, Brazil, where, as confirmed in the *Sentinel* on 23rd April, she arrived safely. On 11th December, 1874, the *Inverugie* was reported "off Deal, from London for Algoa Bay", the trading area for which she had been originally intended. Her stay on the African coast was short-lived. On 12th January, 1876, her owners empowered the captain to "sell the ship for not less than £950, at Hamburg, within one month". He did so and the *Inverugie* thus became less newsworthy locally.

At 95 tons, one of the smaller vessels to leave Francis Robertson's yard, the *Milina* - sometimes called *Malina* (*J3* on page 86) - showed, during a rather adventurous career, that she lacked nothing in the quality of the materials and craftsmanship which went into her building. Her managing-owner was the accountant in the local branch of the Commercial Bank when she was launched on 11th October, 1866, "for the Baltic trade."

For the first few years, her cargoes were mainly cured herrings to one or other of the Baltic ports and coal and lime from Hartlepool and Sunderland to Peterhead. The even tenor of her career was severely interrupted in February, 1872. As readers of the *Sentinel* were informed, "Considerable interest and anxiety was created in the town on Thursday by a telegram which had been received to the effect that the *Milina* had been picked up derelict. In the *Shipping Gazette* we find the following : "The *Melina* (sic) of Peterhead, from Lisbon to Hamburg, with

J3 The Milina.

cargo of minerals and cork, totally dismasted, was picked up on 1st February in Lat 47 Long 7.30 by the *Antagonist*, from Lisbon to London, and towed up the Channel, where she was given up to the Dartmouth tug and taken into Dartmouth. The crew was saved by the *Embla*, barque, of Stavanger." The final part of the report was confirmed two weeks later when a telegram reached Peterhead stating that the crew of the *Milina* had landed at Stavanger the previous day.

Completely refurbished, the *Milina* resumed her normal employment. For example, she sailed from Newcastle for Lisbon on 16th March, 1872 and had made the return trip by 6th May; she then went from Blyth to St. Petersburg and then to London; and, on 7th October, left Leith roads for Lisbon, en route for Mazagan in Morocco. On 18th February, 1873, she arrived in Wexford from Mazagan, proceeded to Swansea, and, by 6th April, was in Lisbon. On her way from Lisbon to Peterhead, she was severely storm-damaged and had to seek shelter in Plymouth. Repaired once again, she continued trading to ports such as Lisbon, Aberdeen, Fraserburgh, London, Danzig, Sunderland, Hamburg, and Pillau until, as reported on 5th December, 1876, she "was towed into Lowestoft with decks swept and considerable other damage, but the crew all safe." Refurbished once more, she was en route from Königsberg to Bergen

when she grounded, during the night, on the sands at Dragor, near Copenhagen. The Master went ashore and made contact with salvors to take the vessel off but a subsequent report informed the owners that the vessel floated off without assistance and proceeded to Bergen, where she arrived on 18th May, 1877.

The *Milina* continued to be chartered for ports in the Baltic until she was sold to a shipowner in Findhorn on 7th January, 1880. On 15th May, 1885, her Registration was closed by direction of the Chief Registrar, "the vessel not having been heard of since 21st February, 1885, when she is supposed to have foundered with all hands on a voyage from Sunderland to the Moray Firth."

On 8th November, 1866, the *Sentinel* produced a typically Victorian purple patch when describing the launch of the *Pitfour*, "A barque as goodly, and strong, and staunch as ever weathered a wintry sea". Built by Stephen and Forbes, she was hailed as "A vessel at once a credit to our town and to our builders. Her model was admired by all as she glided smoothly and safely into her future element amid the huzzas and cheers of the hundreds of onlookers. There is something particularly exciting, noble and grand about witnessing the launch of a goodly vessel. We, as an industrious community, have reason to congratulate ourselves on the many chances of witnessing the numerous vessels, staunch and strong, which are rapidly being launched, and not a few of which are being added to the tonnage of this port. The launch of yesterday was a most successful one; and the vessel, which is of the handsomest proportions, measures:- Tonnage 267; length of keel 109ft (fully 33 metres); breadth 25½ft (slightly less than 8 metres); depth 14ft (fully 4 metres)." Built under special survey, she was classed A1 at Lloyd's for 8 years and was intended for the Mediterranean.

When the *Pitfour* sailed for Newcastle on 21st February, 1867, she "tacked about for some time in the offing, much to the admiration of the maritime critics, who pronounced her sailing powers to be, like her mould and build, first class." As her owners had intended, she was employed mainly between Mediterranean ports such as Palermo, Messina, Patras, Salonica, and Smyrna (Izmir), and New York until 13th September, 1873, when she went ashore on Cape St. Vincent, Portugal, while on passage from Leith to Patras. The vessel became a total wreck but all the crew were saved.

The *Sentinel* informed readers that the North Pier was crowded on Tuesday, 18th June, 1867, to witness "a scene at our harbours, the like of which has not occurred for the past forty-one years, viz. the launching of two vessels in one day from different yards." Immediately after the *Inverary* was launched by Francis Robertson, the 190-ton *Garron* left the ways in the yard belonging to Stephen and Forbes. Named after a creek among the rocks on the seaward side of the East Pier of the North Harbour, her local owners planned to employ her in the Mediterranean trade. Once the rigging out was completed, she sailed for Newcastle, on 24th July, and the *Sentinel* was pleased to report, on 17th January, 1868, that the *Garron* had arrived in Gibraltar "on the 30th day of December, 1867, having made the run from Philadelphia in twenty-one days, beating all the other fruit clippers on the run by four days."

Details of a horrific voyage, made by the *Garron*, were copied from the *Shipping Gazette*. The vessel had sailed from Girgenti, (Agrigento) Sicily, on 20th October, 1871, in fine weather. Five days later, when sixty miles north of Algiers, she encountered a heavy gale and the captain was forced to take the precaution of turning the boat's bow into the wind. In spite of this, the *Garron* was completely dismasted. The crew rigged jury masts and steered a course for Carthagena. On 31st October, the vessel was blown eastwards in another gale and eventually reached Barcelona, after being disabled for fourteen days in the Mediterranean.

By 15th August, 1872, the *Garron* was in Houndeklip Bay, Cape Colony, where the captain and three crewmen narrowly escaped drowning while going ashore in the ship's boat. From Algoa Bay, she sailed to Natal and Calcutta, a far cry from her previous ports of call. The captain was authorised to sell the vessel, for not less than £2,000, in any part of the British Colonies and, in January, 1876, succeeded in doing so in Dunedin, New Zealand.

The 284-ton barque, *Rattray* (*J4* on page 88), was launched by Carnegie and Matthew on 8th February, 1868. Intended for the "Southern trade", she was described as "a clean and well built model with finely tapering lines and handsome bow" with "the requisites in such vessels - speed and cargo capacity." She left Peterhead on 21st March and then sailed on her maiden cargo-carrying voyage on 7th April, 1868, destined for Trinidad with a cargo of coal from Grangemouth. By 13th July, she had returned to Falmouth and by the end of 1868 had sailed from the Clyde to Cadiz and Cartagena, in Spain, whence she went from Malaga to New York. In addition to making at least one other voyage to New York - from Palermo in forty-eight days - the *Rattray* was in ports such as Hamburg, Greenock, Genoa, Gibraltar, Antwerp, Dantzic, and Alloa, before her Peterhead registration was cancelled on 11th February, 1873, after she was sold to a Liverpool owner, who re-named the vessel *Annie Mark*.

When launched from the yard of Stephen and Forbes, on 23rd April, 1868, the 203-ton *Craigewan* (*J5* on page 88) was described, in terms similar to those applied to the *Rattray*, as "a beautiful model of her class with fine tapering lines and clean cut bow, and appears from her construction to combine the maximum of speed with the largest amount of carrying power for her measurement"; she was 111.5 feet (34 metres) long. Ten days later, "The employees of Messrs Stephen and Forbes held a Launch Ball in the Pavilion, Broad Place. The ball was given by the owners on the occasion of the launch of the *Craigewan*. Journeymen and apprentices, with their wives and sweethearts, turned out to enjoy the merry dance which was kept up with energy and spirit far through the morning."

Captain Charles Birnie, formerly Master of the whaler *Xanthus*, was in command when the three-masted schooner left on her maiden voyage. Although the *Craigewan* was "intended for the Southern trade", her first foreign trip, which was reported as "an unprecedented fast run" of three days and twenty hours, was from Dysart, Fife, to Stettin, Poland. From Stettin, she sailed to Christiansand, Norway; then to Newcastle-on-Tyne; then to Vigo in north-west Spain; and then to Malaga in southern Spain, where she arrived within five months of leaving the ways in the Peterhead builders' yard. She

J4 The Rattray.

J5 The Craigewan.

continued to ply the diverse routes of the general trader. For example, she arrived in Boston, U.S.A., from Malaga, on 18th December, 1871 and "passed up the Channel for Antwerp", Belgium, on 10th February, 1872, after leaving Boston thirty days earlier. Later in the same year, the *Craigewan* "cleared at Gibraltar, on 15th July, for Monte Video, Uruguay", where she arrived on 15th September.

In May, 1873, the vessel was sold by public roup in Watt's Inn, Peterhead, for £2,110, to a local family with business interests in Hong Kong and on the China coast but this did not mean that she traded exclusively in the Far East; on 5th October, 1874, for example, she arrived in Stettin from Peterhead.

Captain Birnie was authorised, in February, 1876, to sell the *Craigewan* for not less than £2,600, at any port in China, the Indian Ocean, Australia, or New Zealand. Apart from a voyage to New York, U.S.A., she spent most of the following twelve months in the area around the South China Sea calling in ports such as Bangkok, Thailand; Amoy, China; Tansui, Formosa (Tanshui in Taiwan); and Foochow, China. Having failed to find a buyer for the vessel, Captain Birnie headed homeward via Table Bay, whence he sailed for Falmouth on 10th March, 1877.

The *Craigewan* continued her trading career in European waters. On 18th October, 1877, she arrived in Falmouth, having suffered serious storm-damage during a seven week long voyage from Salonica, (Thessaloniki) Greece. "She lost sails, companion, and skylight; her wheel is broken and everything moveable has been washed off the quarterdeck. The cargo shifted and she is making water. The captain reports that the barque, *Rurik*, of and for Arendal, Norway, with salt, was found in a sinking condition on 11th October and the crew of ten were taken aboard the *Craigewan* and landed at Falmouth." Having been repaired, the *Craigewan* was employed for most of the following year in trading between Dantzic and Hartlepool. A message from Mandal, Norway, reported that she had been in a collision on 1st December, 1878, while on a voyage from Hartlepool with a cargo of coal. There were no casualties among the crew who succeeded in sailing their vessel, "leaking and with heavy damage to her upper works", to Farsund, Norway.

After being repaired, she traded for the following two years "wherever employment could be found." On 6th May, 1879, she was reported to "have passed Elsinore for England"; on 18th October, she had "passed Dover for West"; and on 1st December, was "at Tunis from Hull". In January, 1880, her Master reported that the *Craigewan* had lost her masts in a heavy storm about twenty miles from Cape Carthagena and would require considerable repair.

Rigged out once more, she sailed from Girgenti to Harburg and then to Newcastle. By 7th November, 1880, she had returned from Archangel to Hull and, on 30th November, left for Cette (Sète) on the French Mediterranean coast, where she arrived on 7th January, 1881. During the next five months, she went from St. Margherita in the Caribbean to Hamburg and then to Stockholm, whence she sailed, on 8th June, for Huelva, Spain.

The *Craigewan's* adventurous career came to an end almost within sight of her home port. On the return voyage from Huelva, with a cargo of sulphur ore for Burghead, she ran aground on Forvie Sands, north of the River Ythan estuary, on 26th August, 1881. Captain Birnie was no longer in command. His replacement, Captain Smith, stated that "he did not see a light after he left the English Channel and the weather being thick and the wind blowing directly on the land when he went ashore, he was not sure where he was." The vessel struck between three and four o' clock in the morning. The crew tried to attract attention by burning barrels and all the bedding on board but, after spending two hours in the rigging, they eventually had to abandon ship and reached the shore in the ship's boat. Helped by local salmon fishers, they were able to salvage their personal belongings but the vessel, which was insured, was a total loss.

Carnegie and Matthew launched the *Elderslie*, in September, 1868, for local owners. It was considered worthy of note that all the carved work had been done in the yard by one of the local craftsmen and that, a month after being launched, her first run from Peterhead to Newcastle had been accomplished in twenty-one hours. In spite of being intended for the Brazilian and Mediterranean trade, she was employed extensively in the Far East. Within a period of some twelve months, she left Hong Kong for Bangkok, Thailand, on 7th December, 1871; sailed from Bangkok on the return voyage on 6th February, 1872; sailed again from Hong Kong, on 27th February, for Bangkok and arrived there on 8th March; left Bangkok on 20th March; arrived in Foochow, China, on 4th April; and was in Dunedin, New Zealand, on 14th September, whence she reached Mauritius by 23rd December, 1872. The *Elderslie* was eventually bought by a Melbourne shipowner, in 1873, after being offered for sale for not less than £2,650. A year later, she was registered at Dunedin, New Zealand, having been bought on behalf of merchants based in Oamaru, where she was wrecked in May, 1875.

"The proportion and graceful symmetry of this vessel have been much admired and the careful and elaborate workmanship displayed in her construction, a feature characteristic of all the productions from this firm, is very discernable," commented the

Sentinel, when the first vessel to be built "under a shed" in Peterhead, the 250-ton *Floral Star*, was launched by Stephen and Forbes on 17th November, 1868. Classed 9 years A1 at Lloyd's, the 125 feet (slightly more than 38 metres) boat was intended for general merchant service. She traded between ports in Britain, Europe, South Africa, South America, and Australia before her captain was empowered to sell her for not less than £4,000 at Port Natal, South Africa, or Adelaide, South Australia. She was salvaged and repaired after having run aground at Yankalilla, South Australia, in April, 1875, and was registered in the name of an Australian owner when she was lost on a voyage from Yokohama, Japan, to Newchwang, (Yingkow) China, in April, 1880.

On the same day as the *Sentinel* reported the launch of the *Floral Star*, readers were informed that Stephen and Forbes were going to build another large vessel under cover. The 120 feet (36.5 metres) keel of a clipper schooner, likely to be at least 300 tons, had already been laid. Part of the vessel was to be of larch, which came from Inverness and was "the finest specimen of this wood ever to be imported into Peterhead." When launched on 21st October, 1869, the boat was named *Lord of the Isles* (*J6* below), was 328 tons, and was described as "another of the many splendid clippers which are being turned out in rapid succession from the yard of these enterprising and energetic builders. The mould and the finish of this

their latest essay in naval architecture is perhaps the best." Built for a local firm - which the *Sentinel* congratulated in their endeavours to increase the shipping trade of our port - the vessel was intended to be the first of a line of clippers which would be employed in the China trade.

The *Lord of the Isles* "looked beautifully under canvas and her departure was witnessed by large crowds on the piers" when she left Peterhead on 19th January, 1870, "to load at Newcastle and thence proceed to China." The *Lord of the Isles* traded mainly between Swatow, Shanghai, Amoy, and Hong Kong until, after several attempts to sell the vessel "at China, Japan, or any other place when possible" for between £4,000 and £6,000 had failed, she was eventually sold to a merchant in Chefoo, China, who later sold shares to co-owners from Fife and Woodside, Aberdeen. On 22nd December, 1880, the *Sentinel* relayed a report from Yokohama, Japan, intimating the loss of the *Lord of the Isles* during a storm on 28th September 1880. The crew were rescued by a Russian vessel and landed at Shanghai two months after the *Lord of the Isles* was lost.

Launched on 29th April, 1869, from the yard of Messrs Birnie, one of the smaller local firms, the three-masted, 208-ton *Estelle* was "constructed to carry a large cargo on shallow draft" and was classed 8 years A1 at Lloyd's. She sailed for Aberdeen, in the

J6 *The Lord of the Isles.*

last week of June, to load stones for Galatz on the River Danube, Moldavia. Her owners made good use of her shallow draft, as is well illustrated by her voyages in 1872 and 1873, when she traded to various river ports. Having arrived in Brazil from Liverpool, the *Estelle* sailed from Rio Grande do Norte, on 20th April, 1872; on 9th June, she was reported in lat 29 N long 45 W, and arrived in Falmouth on 6th July. By 15th July, she was in Liverpool, en route for Runcorn on the River Mersey. The *Estelle* left Liverpool, on 29th August, for Rosario, on the River Parana, Argentina, where she arrived on 5th December, after calling at Montevideo, on the River Plate, Uruguay. During 1873, she was again in Rosario and Montevideo and also called at Parana, Argentina; Queenstown, Ireland; and Montrose, Scotland.

The *Estelle* was sold to owners in Liverpool, in 1874 and, later the same year, transferred to Surrey. When a storekeeper in Auckland, New Zealand, was empowered by a Certificate of Sale to dispose of the vessel for not less than £3,000, she was bought by five joint owners - including a draper, a saddler, and a mine manager - in Auckland in June, 1876. She was later transferred to Sydney and, while continuing to work in the Pacific, was subsequently registered in Hamburg. In 1887, the *Estelle* was bought by a Sydney timber merchant who sold her, around the turn of the century, to an Annandale Ferry company to be used as a coal hulk. The company was dissolved in 1904 and, presumably, the *Estelle* was left to rot.

"It is no disparagement to these enterprising builders to say that we think the vessel launched yesterday - in point of model and general rig-out - is the best of several vessels of a similar class and size which they have built since a few years" was the verdict of the *Sentinel*, on 28th May, 1869, when Carnegie and Matthew launched the *Rosebud* for local owners. The second Peterhead-built vessel to be so named, classed A1 for 8 years at Lloyd's, and intended for the Cape trade, she left Peterhead to load coal "for a southern latitude". In addition to return visits to Peterhead, she traded to ports as far apart as London, Table Bay, Singapore, New York, Liverpool, Swinemunde in Poland, Newcastle, Stettin in Poland, Mauritius, and Auckland in New Zealand. A Certificate of Sale, dated 4th November, 1874, empowered an agent of the Union Bank of Australia to sell her, in Melbourne, for not less than £3,300. The *Rosebud* was sold on 31st March, 1875, and, when registered in Melbourne, the managing owner was a grain merchant, who traded in the Far East. In July, 1880, she "was sold foreign, at Nagasaki", Japan.

When Stephen and Forbes launched the 189-ton *Vixen* on 27th September, 1870, she was described as "a finely modelled three-masted schooner to be employed in the fruit trade." Following the practice of "going where employment could be found", her charters took her from Malaga to Baltimore; Cardiff to Naples and return; Cardiff to Mazagan; Casablanca to Liverpool; Liverpool to Pernambuco, Brazil; Baltimore to Cardiff with grain; Table Bay to Guam; Adelaide to Table Bay; Fraserburgh to Hamburg; Liverpool to Fraserburgh; Newcastle to Barletta in Italy and Odessa on the Black Sea; Gioia in southern Italy to Hull; and Dantzic to Peterhead.

On 5th January, 1881, the *Sentinel* reported that "the *Vixen* had put into port severely damaged having had part of her maintopmast and her mizzentopmast carried away. The Captain states that his vessel sustained the damage on Friday afternoon in a strong gale when 70 miles off Flamborough Head. The sea at the time was rolling so heavy that the gear had to be cut in order to clear the mast from the ship. The *Vixen* was on passage from Uddevalla, Sweden, to Bo'ness with a cargo of wood. The damage is to be repaired here." Once the damage was repaired, the *Vixen* continued her normal employment and on 5th May, 1881, arrived in Palermo from Newcastle. Some shares in the vessel were exposed for sale, by public auction, in the Royal Hotel, Peterhead, in January, 1883, but there were no bidders. The *Vixen* was eventually sold to a shipowner in Cornwall on 1st April, 1884.

A week before Christmas, 1871, Stephen and Forbes launched another vessel for the firm for which they had built the *Lord of the Isles*. Like her predecessor, the three-masted schooner, the *Jessie McDonald*, 300 tons and 123 feet (37.5 metres), was also intended for the China coasting trade. After leaving Peterhead for Newcastle, on 21st February, 1872, she sailed for Penang, Malaya, and commenced trading along the well-established routes in the China Seas and Australasia; by the end of the year, she had called at Hong Kong, Amoy, and Foochow, before heading for Sydney. Two years later, on 11th November, the *Sentinel* was very pleased to announce that one of the owners in Peterhead had "received a letter from the Harbour Master, Hong Kong, intimating that he had received a communication from the British Consul at Yokohama stating that the Japanese Government had handed him 100 golden guilders to be paid to Captain Sievewright of the schooner, *Jessie McDonald*, as a reward for his humanity in rescuing 3 Japanese fishermen in March." The vessel continued to trade between ports such as Shanghai, Hong Kong, Newchwang (Yingkow), Sydney, Foochow, Adelaide, Newcastle in New South Wales, Natal, and London. On 30th December, 1880, she arrived at Table Bay from Inhambane, Mozambique,; sailed from Table Bay on 2nd February, 1881; and, by 21st April, had left Flushing for Rotterdam. On 9th May, she was reported to be off Dungeness, heading west; on 7th October, she "crossed Natal bar, drawing thirteen and a half feet" (slightly more than four metres), en route for Batavia, where she arrived on 17th December, 1881. A year later, the *Jessie McDonald* had been sold to Irish owners who transferred her to the *Belfast Registry* on 1st December, 1882.

The 191-ton *Olive Branch*, "a very handsome three-masted schooner, the property of local owners," was launched from the yard of Messrs Carnegie and Matthew on 23rd July, 1872. During the next ten years, without appearing in any spectacular headlines, she acquitted herself very handsomely, as the local cognoscenti had predicted, on the trans-continental trade routes. In constant employment, her copybook career must have been the envy of many owners, captains, and crews.

She left Peterhead on 10th September, 1872, on her maiden voyage, with barrels of cured herrings for Stettin where she shipped a cargo for Buenos Aires; she was reported passing Elsinore, westward, on 16th October, and reached the Rio de la Plata on Hogmanay. By 25th May, 1873, the *Olive Branch* had re-crossed the Atlantic to Queenstown, en route for Hamburg, where she arrived on 13th June. She was then chartered for a four-week long voyage, in the month of July, carrying a cargo from Antwerp to Archangel, whence she returned, via London, to her home port after a very satisfactory first season.

The *Olive Branch* sailed from Peterhead in October, 1873. During the next two years, apart from Peterhead, her ports of call included Stettin, Dantzic, Ostend, Leghorn (*J7* below), Archangel, St. Vincent in the West Indies, London, Jamaica, Copenhagen, and Dundee. New destinations were added annually to her charters; for example, in 1876, Lisbon and Cuxhaven; in 1877, Gallipoli, Corfu, and Naples; in 1878, Guadeloupe; and in 1879, Martinique and St. Nazaire.

Between September, 1879 - when she left Peterhead for Dantzic with a cargo of cured herrings - and August, 1881, the *Olive Branch* undertook more long-distance charters than ever before. She sailed from Peterhead to Libau (Liepaja in Latvia); from Libau to London; from London to Kingston, Jamaica, and back again; to Natal; to Port Pirie, Australia, and back to Natal; from Natal, via St. Helena, to the West Indies; and to London from the West Indies.

After being sold to a shipowner in Bridport Harbour, Dorset, her Registration was transferred to London on 29th January, 1883, and her name changed to *Phyllis Gray*. She was wrecked in the winter of 1908.

In the presence of the Earl and Countess of Erroll from Slains Castle and Colonel and Mrs. Ferguson from Pitfour, Stephen and Forbes launched the

J7 From a painting : "Olive Branch of Peterhead, Captain James Collie, entering Leghorn Feb. 24th, 1874."

J8 The Countess of Erroll "rigging out" soon after being launched.

Countess of Erroll (*J8 above*) on 29th January, 1873. Classed A1 at Lloyd's for 9 years, the 180-ton, three-masted schooner was built for the Mediterranean trade but was not employed as intended. Seven weeks after being launched, she left Peterhead, in ballast, for Granton. She had returned from Riga, Latvia, to Arbroath by 11th June and, in another six weeks, she was in Peterhead Bay, about to sail for China. She was reported to have left Foochow, China, for Melbourne, Australia, on 10th October, 1874, and thereafter, apart from brief visits to European waters, most of her ports of call were located between the Cape of Good Hope and New Zealand. For example, she sailed from Peterhead on 1st, April, 1876, for Shields; left Newcastle for Table Bay three months later; and, on 14th August, sailed from Table Bay for Mauritius. She then called at Otago, New Zealand, and sailed for Melbourne, on 8th January, 1877. Her next port of call was Colombo, Ceylon (Sri Lanka), where she arrived on 20th April. She left for Singapore on 5th June and was in Shanghai on 18th August. The *Countess of Erroll* arrived in Otago from Foochow, China, on 11th January, 1878; reached Newcastle, New South Wales, from Dunedin, New Zealand, on 20th March; arrived in Hong Kong from Newcastle, New South Wales, on 28th May; returned to Foochow; and sailed for Dunedin on 23rd July, 1878. By 22nd July, 1879,

the *Countess of Erroll* had returned to Queenstown, Ireland, from Mauritius, and, four days later, was on her way to London. She "cleared at London, on 11th November, 1879, for Natal", where she arrived on 11th February, 1880; left on 30th March; and arrived in Calcutta on 6th May. The *Countess of Erroll* continued to trade between Natal and Calcutta until, after returning to the former on 20th March, 1881, she sailed for the West Indies to load sugar for Greenock. She was in St. Helena on 20th April and reached Barbados on 31st May.

She was sold on 22nd September, 1884, through the agency of the City of London Bank, to a coal merchant in Sydney. He used her in the coastal and the trans-Tasman coal trade until she was damaged by heavy weather in the Tasman Sea on 29th September, 1907. The *Countess of Erroll* was then sold for use as a hulk and was beached in Evans Bay, Wellington, New Zealand, until 1934, when she was broken up, over sixty years after being launched in such prestigious company in Peterhead.

Less than four months after the *Countess of Erroll* left Peterhead on her maiden voyage, Stephen and Forbes launched another three-masted schooner, the 186-ton *Tullochgorum*, which had almost the same dimensions as her predecessor on the ways. Early in her career, she traded between such places as Hull, Gibraltar, Archangel, Newcastle, Corfu, Stettin, and Peterhead. The *Tullochgorum* also carried freight in the Indian Ocean and in Australasian waters. On 17th May, 1876, for example, she arrived in Littleton, New Zealand, from Mauritius, and then proceeded to Adelaide. By 26th October, she had reached Newcastle, New South Wales, from Sydney, and arrived in Hong Kong on Christmas Day, 1876. She continued to trade between Hong Kong, Foochow, and Melbourne, where she arrived on 19th November, 1877. After a voyage to Natal, she returned to Melbourne on 27th April, 1878; proceeded along the Australian coast to Maryleborough; and then "cleared at Melbourne with a cargo of bone dust for Mauritius" on 19th August, 1878. On 2nd November, she was towed into Port Louis with her cargo on fire due to spontaneous combustion. Once the fire was extinguished, the vessel was repaired and resumed her normal employment. She returned to Australia and left Newcastle, New South Wales, for Port Pirie, north of Adelaide, on 21st April, 1879. The *Tullochgorum* then sailed to Batavia before returning to Newcastle, New South Wales, on 16th October. She left Newcastle for Adelaide on 31st October, 1879; carried on to Port Augusta, South Australia, and then headed for England. Her next reported position was 30 S and 35 E; on 1st May, she was "off the Lizard, en route for Falmouth for orders"; and, on 5th June, 1880, she was in Rouen. The *Tullochgorum* was reported "off Gibraltar" on 1st November; at London on 21st November; and, on a rare visit to her home port, in Peterhead, on 29th December, 1880. In the following year, she sailed from Peterhead to Blyth; then to Messina, where she arrived on 13th June; and, after a trip to the Baltic, left Stettin for Brest on 7th December. The *Tullochgorum* was eventually sold to a ship owner in Pentewan, Cornwall, in July, 1896.

The 228-ton *Lochiel*, with "the bust of a Highland chieftain, very tastefully cut and painted" as a figurehead, was another three-masted schooner which became a familiar sight in the main ports between Cape Town and New Zealand. Intended for the "general trade" when launched from the yard of Stephen and Forbes, in February, 1875, she was commanded by Captain Ewan, formerly of the *Princess of Wales*, as she crossed and re-crossed the oceans between Table Bay, Newchwang (Yingkow), Hong Kong, Adelaide, Mauritius, Otago, Sydney, Launceston, Port Pirie, Littleton, Melbourne, and Newcastle, New South Wales.

Readers of the *Buchan Observer* learned that the *Wandering Minstrel* had been launched on 20th July, 1875. Built under special survey for local owners, copper-fastened, and with iron hold beams, the 362-ton, three-masted barque was classed 10 years A1

at Lloyd's. Intended for the China trade, she was the biggest vessel built by Stephen and Forbes and was to be commanded by the former Master of the *Jessie McDonald*, who had "hit the headlines" in November, 1874, with the announcement that the British Consul at Yokohama had received one hundred golden guilders, from the Japanese Government, "to be paid to Captain Sievewright of the schooner *Jessie McDonald* as a reward for his humanity in rescuing three Japanese fishermen in March."

Captain Sievewright took his new command out of Peterhead on 24th November, 1875. The *Buchan Observer* relayed a report from Melbourne that the *Wandering Minstrel* had returned there for repairs, after being extensively damaged while at anchor at Port Philip heads on 1st February, 1878. Having been repaired, the vessel returned to the China coasting trade and arrived in Melbourne from Foochow on 8th November, 1878. In the following year, the *Sentinel*, quoting the *Overland China Mail* of 3rd June, informed its readers that the *Wandering Minstrel* had experienced very severe weather while on a voyage from Takao in Formosa (Kaohsiung in Taiwan) to Hong Kong with a cargo of sugar. The vessel had been caught in a typhoon and had all her sails blown away. Seaworthy once more, she returned to familiar waters. On 19th October, 1879, she left Foochow for Melbourne, where she arrived on 29th December. On 28th January, 1880, she left Melbourne for Newcastle, New South Wales, "to load for Hong Kong". The voyage from Newcastle to Hong Kong lasted from 25th February until 13th April, 1880; on 3rd November, she arrived in Algoa Bay from Foochow; on 4th December, she was at Cape Town; and on Christmas Day, 1880, left East London, Cape Province, for Mauritius.

On 9th March, 1881, the *Sentinel* reported that the owners in Peterhead had received a Lloyd's telegram from Calcutta stating that it was "feared that the barque, *Wandering Minstrel*, of Peterhead, about eighty days from Table Bay, had been lost in a cyclone at the Mauritius." Readers learned that the vessel had been employed almost exclusively in the Australian and China trade and had left Table Bay, on 14th December, 1880, in ballast for Calcutta, to load rice for the return voyage to Cape Town. The paper added that, apart from the captain and the twenty-two years old mate, all the crew were believed to be Chinamen! Fortunately, another telegram was received advising the owners of the safe arrival of the vessel and crew in Calcutta on 11th March. By 10th June, 1881, she had left Algoa Bay on the return voyage to Table Bay and, having sailed east once again, called at Madras before returning to Natal on 19th August.

As far as Peterhead was concerned, the colourful

career of the *Wandering Minstrel* came to an end when she was sold to a merchant in Victoria, Hong Kong, where she was registered on 5th June, 1885.

On 26th April, 1876, there was a report in the *Sentinel* that "On the evening of Friday last, carpenters in the employment of Carnegie and Matthew were treated to a ball, on the occasion of the launching of the *Rosebud*, when about thirty couples assembled in the Pavilion, at 8 o'clock, where they danced with spirit and great good will until far through the morning of Saturday. Captain Collie, Master of the *Rosebud*, the owners, and the builders, who gave the ball, honoured it with their presence. With Mr. G. Birnie as M.C., and a band under Mr. John Gunn, the whole proceedings went off well."

The second vessel with this name to be launched by Carnegie and Matthew, the *Rosebud* (*J9* below), at 352 tons register, was the biggest they ever built and was intended for the Cape and China trade. Once in her working environment, she followed a pattern of trade which led her to ports of call frequented by several other Peterhead-built vessels. For example, having left Peterhead for her maiden voyage, on 7th June, 1876, she shipped cargo in Newcastle and sailed for Cape Town on 24th June. By 30th July, she was in lat 12 N long 25 W and arrived in Cape Town on 7th September. Continuing eastward, she left Table Bay on 2nd October and arrived in Calcutta on 23rd November. On the return voyage, she sailed from Calcutta to Algoa Bay in forty-two days and, ten days later, sailed from Port Elizabeth for Table Bay, where she anchored on 20th February, 1877. She left Table Bay bound for Adelaide, on 7th March, and, after returning to Cape Province, left again, on 7th August for Melbourne, where she arrived on 15th October. Less than four weeks later, she was en route for Colombo and, by 18th April, 1878, had returned to Melbourne and was on her way to Sydney.

The *Rosebud* left Newcastle, New South Wales, on 17th May, 1878, for Hong Kong, where she arrived on 13th July. She then sailed for Foochow and arrived on 25th July. She remained there until 29th September, when she left for Australia and reached Melbourne, Victoria, on 15th December. On 26th January, 1879, she arrived in Fremantle, Western Australia; was in Hong Kong on 19th April; and sailed for Takao, Formosa, (Kaohsiung, Taiwan) on 21st May. She sailed from Hong Kong for Whampoa, China, on 26th September; continued to Newchwang (Yingkow) and returned to Hong Kong on 11th October; and left for London on 23rd October. On the return voyage to Natal, the *Rosebud* was reported off Deal on 9th April, 1880, and, after an

J9 From a painting : the Rosebud at Hong Kong.

95

exceptionally slow passage, was off the Isle of Wight seventeen days later. She arrived in Natal on 5th July and, on 3rd October, left for Newcastle, New South Wales. She reached there on 17th November and then proceeded to Shanghai, where she arrived on 11th February, 1881. The *Rosebud* then made a round trip from Shanghai to Nagasaki, Japan, before sailing for New York, via St. Helena. She was reported to be in Great Yarmouth on 1st January, 1882; to have arrived at Port Louis, Mauritius, from Cape Town, on 29th August; and to have sailed for Launceston, Tasmania, on 3rd October, 1882. On 13th September, 1883, she was at St. Helena, on her way from Formosa to Halifax, Nova Scotia; on 24th March, 1884, she left Whitehaven for Buenos Aires; and on 18th August, 1884, arrived in Rosario from San Nicolas, both ports on the River Parana in Argentina.

The *Rosebud* was wrecked at Mossel Bay (Mosselbaai, Cape Province) on 30th August, 1888. The Certificates of Competency of both Master and Mate were confiscated. During a subsequent Inquiry into the stranding, it transpired that the vessel had arrived at Calcutta from Port Natal, on 11th June, and had left Calcutta with a crew of ten and six passengers, on 1st July, after shipping a full cargo for Cape Town and Mossel Bay, where she arrived on 26th August. It was impossible to discharge any cargo until 29th August. On that night, there was a terrific gale and, since the vessel was in imminent danger, Captain Collie decided to run the vessel on shore in order to save those on board. The finding of the Court of Inquiry was that the loss of the boat, which was perfectly seaworthy, was not occasioned by any fault on the part of the master. His Certificate was returned to him, as was the mate's. The *Rosebud* was only partially insured and the *Buchan Observer*, making no comment about his putting the safety of the crew above his own financial interests, simply concluded that "Captain Collie (who was also part-owner) will be a heavy loser."

"Peterhead Ships at the Antipodes"

Some of the largest merchant vessels launched from yards in Peterhead were built expressly to be employed mainly in antipodean waters. The 320-ton *Leonidas* was the first of several Robertson-built boats, which established his firm's reputation in Australia and New Zealand. Launched in 1854, she traded between Newcastle, New South Wales; Melbourne; Port Louis, Mauritius; and Otago, New Zealand, before two shipping agents in Sydney were empowered by a Certificate of Sale on 20th February, 1862, to sell the vessel within twelve months, for not less than £2,750. She was bought two months later by a Sydney shipowner, a member of a colliery-owning family, and was employed carrying

coals from Newcastle, New South Wales, for the next four years. She was then sold to a firm which traded among the South Sea Islands and was wrecked on Toomba Reef, Bulari Pass, New Caledonia, on 2nd June, 1873; a far cry from the building-yard at Brook Lane on the north-east shoulder of old Caledonia!

On 19th February, 1858, the *Sentinel* published the following parody on a song popular in the Scottish Borders :-

The Bonnie Yarrow
Tune *Braes o' Yarrow*

There's braw, braw ships frae our ain port -
Our Greenland fleet there's few can marra',
But what think ye o' the new launch'd craft,
The handsome, trim-built, bonnie Yarrow?

There's bigger ships, nae doubt, afloat,
And clipper crafts as fleet's an arrow,
But I ne'er saw a ship before
Glide down to the deep like the bonnie Yarrow.

Luck to the craft where'er she goes,
May she aye keep aff frae rock and shallow;
Luck o' guide winds, o' tides and freights,
Aye attend the bonnie Yarrow.

Then here's for luck, wi' three times three,
To the fastest ship may she prove a marra'.
"Never Say Die" let her motto be,
And nail't to the mast o' the bonnie Yarrow.

The editor explained that he had received it from "an admirer" when, "On Tuesday last, amid the rejoicings usual on such occasions, a compactly built schooner was launched from the building yard of Mr. Francis Robertson. The vessel is 185 tons, builder's measurement, and is to be engaged in the Australian trade. She is owned by Mr. T.E. Mitchell and will be commanded by Captain Matheson, late of the *Mary Russell* of Dundee. The vessel has been named the *Yarrow* and, the ceremony having been tastefully performed, this worthy addition to our tonnage glided beautifully into the water, while the well-wishes of the crowd - success to the *Yarrow* - received a loud and hearty expression."

The *Yarrow* was commonly known in the Antipodes as the *Yarra*. When she sailed from Peterhead in the middle of April, 1858, she was pronounced "a fine looking craft" which would "no doubt, give a good account of this her first trip." She did; and continued to do so for the next sixteen years.

James Matheson, Master of the *Yarra* on her maiden voyage, owned eight shares of the vessel - one eighth of the total. He was born in Peterhead on 2nd March,

1823, the son of Captain Thomas Matheson, and, continuing the family seafaring tradition, began a four-year apprenticeship in the *Lydia* of Peterhead, in July, 1839. After serving as Mate in several vessels, he gained his Certificate of Competency as Master, which was issued, on 18th August, 1854, at Peterhead, where his address was in the Longate. He had married Christina Weir, Mill of Philorth, Fraserburgh, on 14th January, 1850, and, leaving their three years old son, James, with the Mathesons in Peterhead, she sailed with him when, as recorded in the ship's log, the *Yarra* embarked on "a voyage to Port Natal and thence as required to any other port or place in the Cape Colonies, North and South Pacific Oceans, India and China Seas and Straits, and the Australian Colonies, as employment may be found." (James Matheson, Junior, did not sail for New Zealand to join his parents until 1870, but died on board ship before the vessel docked.)

Mrs. Matheson's second son, John, was born aboard the *Yarra* in Port Louis, Mauritius, on 21st November, 1858. A fortnight later, laden with sugar, the *Yarra* sailed for Adelaide. In keeping with the usual practice, enough water had been taken aboard to provide the daily rations for the crew and the captain's wife but the baby had not been included in the calculations; he was expected to share his parents' meagre allowance! (John lived for eighty-three years, without requiring any hospital treatment, after deriving most of his nourishment from sugar cane for the first six weeks of his life!!)

When crossing the Indian Ocean, Captain Matheson fell ill with malaria and the Mate broke his leg in an accident. Fortunately, Mrs. Matheson had taken an interest in navigation and was sufficiently proficient to steer the required course. Nothing daunted, although she was nursing her weeks-old son, she assumed command of the *Yarra*. The crew were on the verge of mutiny, mainly because of a very poor diet, and so she supplemented their ration with a kind of dried plum. This proved effective as long as the plums lasted but when her supply was exhausted it was her resourcefulness, sheer force of personality, and a dour, dogged determination, derived from Buchan roots, which enabled her to keep the crew under control and pilot the *Yarra* safely to her destination.

This was not the last of the *Yarra's* eventful voyages. Captain Matheson continued trading between Mauritius and Australian ports, gaining Pilot Exemption Certificates for Melbourne, Geelong, and Launceston, in 1859, and Sydney, Newcastle, and Twofold Bay, in 1860. On one occasion, the crew deserted at Adelaide and joined in the rush to the Victorian goldfield. Captain Matheson tied up his boat and followed them. He soon decided that his

prospects were worse as a miner than as Master of his own boat and so he returned to his ship, and recruited a crew of equally disillusioned, would-be gold millionaires.

On another occasion, the *Yarra* was on passage from Launceston, Tasmania, to Mauritius and, on 18th January, 1860, was five days out from Port Louis. An eerie calm, extremely oppressive atmosphere, and rapidly falling barometer warned Captain Matheson of an impending storm. He ordered all sails to be taken in, with the exception of a small jury rig sufficient to give steerage way, and all hatches were made doubly secure. On the morning of 20th January, the storm broke with the full fury of an Indian Ocean hurricane and the crew was ordered below. The steering-wheel was in the open with next to no protection from the elements and so the helmsman had been lashed to the stanchion of the wheel. The captain replaced the helmsman for a time but eventually was forced to lash the wheel and to take refuge below deck where the galley fire had been extinguished and so the crew had to survive on "hard tack" and water. The *Yarra* was in the vortex of the hurricane and the crew was compelled to remain below for six days, in almost continuous darkness and with very little to eat, while the boat pitched and rolled and the wind howled through the remains of the rigging. When the men returned to the deck, they found ample evidence of the excellent quality of the materials and the high standard of craftsmanship which had gone into the building of their vessel for the *Yarra* had survived without being dismasted. After the crew had made the necessary running repairs, the *Yarra* arrived safely in Port Louis on 31st January, 1860.

Once the damage had been repaired and a cargo shipped, the *Yarra* left Port Louis on 14th March, 1860, en route for Melbourne, where she arrived without further mishap. Captain Matheson wished to have some visible record of his boat in the storm and so he gave a detailed description of his experience to an artist he had commissioned to create an "artist's eye" view of the *Yarra* in the vortex of the hurricane. This was done and two artist's impressions were produced. (Both are still extant in the possession of Captain Matheson's great grandson, Wayne Matheson, to whom we are grateful for information about the *Yarra* and for the copy (*J10* on page 98) of one of the paintings of the vessel in the vortex of the hurricane. Wayne Matheson is the Executive Director of a timber firm based in the premises, in Invercargill, New Zealand, formerly occupied by a woolscouring firm established by his grandfather, John, the boy born on the *Yarra*, in Port Louis, Mauritius, in 1858!

James Royce, a Wesleyan missionary, embarked on

J10 From a painting : "Yarra in the vortex of a hurricane, Lat 20°46'S Long 77°1'E, 26/1/1862."

the *Yarra*, on 17th June, 1861, to sail from Fiji to Sydney to seek medical advice regarding the possibility of having a finger amputated. In his diary, he described how "a gale set in right ahead which kept us some days at a standstill, the wheel was tied up and the ship hove to while a tremendous sea was running. At length the wind veered round.....and raised expectations of a speedy arrival, but we found on Monday that a strong current had taken us some sixty miles out of our course to the leeward of Lord Howe's Island, under which we passed very close, and it was a merciful providence which saved us from running upon it in the dark. ..... The vessel we are in is a topsail schooner of one hundred and twenty tons, almost new, built of oak, and said to be very strong..... In consequence of the rough weather and the inconvenient smallness of the ship, our facilities for religious worship have been anything but what one could wish; in fact it has been quite a chasm in one's religious history which I trust may never occur again ..... our passage from Fiji has been rough and tedious, extending over some thirty-two days; we did not anchor in Sydney harbour until Friday the 19th. ..... This morning (Monday, 22nd July, 1861) I went to our vessel to see our trunks off and found that the captain was very ill, having taken a severe cold during the voyage."

(Captain Matheson recovered and, after selling his share of the *Yarra* on 28th August, 1861, purchased another boat and sailed to New Zealand, hoping to take advantage of the Otago gold rush. He was involved in the lightering business between Port Chalmers and Dunedin and in the coasting trade among the West Coast gold towns before becoming Assistant Harbourmaster at Kakanui in April, 1868.)

Meanwhile, the *Yarra* had continued her adventurous career. She was wrecked at Wanganui, New Zealand, in July, 1865; was sold, repaired, and registered at Wellington; and then, in 1868, sold again to a Sydney owner who employed her along the east coast of Australia. She was bound for Sydney, with a cargo of coal and coke, when her crew abandoned her during a violent storm. They reached the shore safely but the *Yarra* was finally wrecked on North Beach (now known as Stockton Beach) Newcastle, New South Wales, on 1st February, 1874.

The next vessel built by Francis Robertson for the antipodean trade was much bigger than the *Yarra* and better equipped for carrying passengers. Launched on 17th April, 1862, the *Charlotte Andrews* was described as "a magnificent barque of the clipper mould..... She is 465 tons builders' old measurement -

356 N.M.(New Measurement) - and is being fitted with Cunningham's self-reefing topsails (the first vessel so fitted here). Her inside space is tastefully and usefully laid off. With large carrying accommodation, her fore and after cabins possess considerable available room for passengers - her fore cabin (which is elegantly fitted up) containing four passenger berths and her after cabin eight double berths."

(With Cunningham's self-reefing topsails, there was no need for members of the crew to climb into the rigging to tie up the reef-points on the sails when it was necessary to reduce the surface area exposed to the wind. This could be done from the deck by means of double halyards fitted in such a manner that on lowering one of them the topsail yard was made to revolve and roll the sail round it. In spite of this obvious advantage, several "old salts" were reluctant to use the newfangled method when Cunningham had patented his invention some years earlier; they said it would transform sailors to maids rolling up blinds!)

The *Charlotte Andrews* left Peterhead for London, on 24th May, prior to her maiden voyage to Australia. Shipping agents in Sydney were empowered to sell her for not less than £4,500 and after they did so in November, 1862, the *Charlotte Andrews* traded in antipodean waters for the remainder of her career.

The *Sentinel*, on 23rd January, 1863, reported her arrival in Sydney in considerable detail. "She made a very quick passage and has beat one of the fastest clippers on the sea (which sailed at the same time) by nearly three weeks. The captain states she is a very fast vessel and will sail over eleven knots an hour close hauled to the wind. He also says that his log-reel contained only twelve and a half knots and she frequently bawled it off long before our log-glass was out." The captain reckoned "that she will sail thirteen knots or over; but we never had a good day's run - the same never continuing for 24 hours - the barque is a good sea-boat and is very dry." The *Sentinel*, aware of the keen interest in the details of the vessel's performance, quoted from two separate editions of the *Sydney Morning Herald* : "This clipper barque will prove a valuable addition to the list of colonial vessels.... She sailed from the Downs on 27th June but when off Cape Finisterre sprang her foremast and had to bear up on 8th July and arrived at Falmouth on the 16th. She sailed again on 20th July; crossed the equator on 17th August and the meridian of the Cape on 10th September; ran down her easting in Latitude 41 degrees; and was off Cape Leeuwin on 3rd inst. - 74 days out from thence. She had head winds and calms to Cape Otway..... This fine clipper barque which arrived from England a few weeks since, has been laid on for San Francisco for which port she will sail in a week. Her cabin and steerage accommodations are very superior and offer an excellent opportunity for passengers and being a very fast vessel, she will doubtless make a rapid passage. With all this, we think that Peterhead may well be proud of her shipbuilders." In the light of this panegyric, the editor of the *Sentinel* could not resist a parting comment, "Things are looking up for us when we can meet the famed Aberdeen clippers on their own ground" and it was this, and similar eulogies, which led him to extol the skills of the Peterhead shipbuilders when he wrote *The Howes o' Buchan*.

On 1st January, 1864, under the heading - A FEATHER IN THE CAP OF THE PETERHEADIANS : THE *CHARLOTTE ANDREWS* BEATING A GOVERNMENT MAIL STEAMER, the *Sentinel* relayed the following from an Auckland newspaper dated 26th September, 1863, "The *Charlotte Andrews*, a new and truly handsome little clipper barque, hailing from Sydney but built in Peterhead, unexpectedly made her appearance from Sydney on Monday last, after a smart run of seven and a half days, having anticipated the English mail by a day. She brought one hundred and nineteen of the Waikato military settlers." In spite of the vessel's "cabin and steerage accommodations" being "very superior", the living conditions of such a number must have been very uncomfortable!

The *Sentinel* made no attempt to explain the intriguing reference to the Waikato military settlers and so his readers remained ignorant of the small part played by the *Charlotte Andrews* in the creation of a British Empire on which the sun never set. As a temporary troop-ship, she had become involved, indirectly, in one of the thirteen minor "wars" which occurred when the British were trying to subjugate the Maoris. The latter objected when, in 1862, the New Zealand Governor, George Grey, organised the building of a road to facilitate access from Auckland to the Waikato River. They thought this was bound to lead to more white settlers arriving to confiscate land belonging to natives and so they ordered all Europeans to leave the area and threatened to ravage the settlement of Auckland. In July, 1863, the British Commander-in-Chief, Sir Duncan Cameron, ordered some of his regular troops to invade the Waikato to keep the Maoris under control. The Auckland Militia was mobilised and this caused an acute shortage of labour in the Province.

The New Zealand Government proposed that a system of military settlements should be established on land confiscated from the warring tribes. Initial attempts to attract disillusioned miners from the Otago gold fields failed and so it was decided to enlist recruits from Australia. Eleven vessels, including the *Charlotte Andrews*, were chartered to transport the recruits and their families across the Tasman Sea and by the end of October, 1863, the Waikato Militia numbered more than two thousand.

On boarding the transport vessels in Australia, each recruit was issued with a pair of blankets, a knife, fork, spoon, tin plate, and pannikin. When they arrived at Auckland, recruits were marched to a barracks where they were issued with two pairs of blue trousers with a red stripe down each leg, two blue serge jumpers, two pairs of boots, a round forage cap, and their arms. After their training was complete, they were stationed in the various redoubts scattered throughout the district. Militiamen were paid according to rank. The daily rate for a Captain was 11s.7d (57½p); for a Sergeant 3s.6d (17½p); and for a Private 2s.6d (12½p).

It is interesting to note some of the terms and conditions associated with the Waikato military settlements, which were located on sites selected by the Government for their strategic importance in the struggle against the Maoris. Each settlement was to consist of not less than one hundred town allotments, each of which measured one acre, and one hundred farm sections. Settlers undertook to serve for three years in the Militia in exchange for a grant of a town allotment and a farm section, the size of which was determined on the basis of rank; for example, a Captain received 300 acres (about 121 hectares); a Sergeant 80 acres (about 32 hectares); and a Private 50 acres (about 20 hectares). For the first year after taking possession of their allotments, settlers, who were allowed to retain their weapons, accoutrements, and ammunition, were entitled to receive rations on the same scale as supplied to Her Majesty's troops.

The *Charlotte Andrews* was eventually bought by a firm involved in the timber business and was on her way to load a cargo of logs for Sydney when she dragged her anchors in Ramsay Bay, Queensland, on 6th October, 1879. She grounded and broke up soon afterwards. The remains of the vessel, which cost at least £4,500 when it arrived in Sydney more than sixteen years earlier, were sold at public auction for £6! A subsequent Inquiry blamed the Master for her loss and suspended his Certificate for three months.

Francis Robertson's yard had acquired a reputation for building boats which were eminently suitable for the antipodean trade and the Forth and New Zealand Shipping Company placed an order for the first of a line of vessels with which they planned to carry on a regular trade between Leith and New Zealand. Launched on 1st June, 1863, the *Prospector* was described as "a fine clipper barque of 236 tons N.M.. She is 120 feet long (about 36.5 metres), 27½ feet broad (about 8.4 metres), and 12½ feet (about 3.8 metres) deep and is a beautiful model of a vessel. She is fitted with every modern improvement and has spacious passenger accommodation."

Within four weeks of being launched, the *Prospector* left Peterhead and, after loading at "the Leith berth for New Zealand", sailed on her maiden voyage on 13th August. On 18th January, 1864, the *Otago Times* reported that "the barque, *Prospector*, the pioneer of the Forth and New Zealand Shipping Company's vessels, after discharging part of her cargo at Invercargill, proceeded direct to Dunedin Bay, having been purposely built for entering the shallow waters of New Zealand ports. She was the first home vessel to enter the New River (after a passage of ninety-five days) direct from home and the first of the east of Scotland traders to arrive in the Port of Otago."

A year later, the *Prospector* made the fastest passage on record between Port Chalmers, north of Dunedin, and Valparaiso, "the distance from port to port (something over 5,000 miles) being run in twenty-seven days." The previous record was 35 days and "it is worthy of note as showing the sailing capabilities of the ship, that the first 3,000 miles were run in eleven days and that during the voyage she had to contend with four successive days of light baffling winds and a strong contrary current."

After being sold by the Forth and New Zealand Shipping Company, the *Prospector*, although mortgaged to the Bank of Otago for £3,000, was registered in Dunedin in the name of Captain James Duncan, a native of Arbroath who had become a shipowner after emigrating to New Zealand. She was employed as a wool ship and the seafaring fraternity in Peterhead were kept informed of the high points in her career. The *Sentinel*, quoting from the *Oamaru Times*, reported that she had "out-sailed the *Star of Tasmania*, one of the Aberdeen-built clippers." The same paper chronicled some of her remarkable runs between ports such as San Francisco, Auckland, Port Chalmers, Valparaiso, San Antonio, Otago, and Port Louis. It highlighted the fact that she had sailed from Cape Horn to the Cape of Good Hope, 4,500 miles in nineteen days, and had covered 75,000 miles in the previous twenty-four months, for nine of which she had been tied up in port.

The *Prospector* was bought by a shipowner in Newcastle, New South Wales, in 1877. She was employed as a coastal collier for the next seven years and was then purchased by the New South Wales Government and used to store explosives. Her entry in the *Register of Shipping* was not closed until 1919, fifty-six years after leaving Peterhead, when "no trace of the vessel could be found"!

Less than ten months after the *Prospector* was launched, another vessel for the Forth and New

Zealand Shipping Company left the ways in Francis Robertson's yard. The *Southland* was "especially fitted up as a passenger vessel - her accommodation in this respect being exceedingly ample" and, although 34 tons heavier, her dimensions were almost identical to those of the *Prospector*. To celebrate the launch, "carpenters and others connected with the building and outfitting of the *Southland* (with their wives and sweethearts) were entertained by Mr. Robertson at a ball in the Pavilion, Broad Place. The company was a large one and dancing (commenced at half-past eight) was carried on till the daylight of the morning chased away the gay revellers."

The *Otago Times*, in reporting the arrival of the *Southland* in New Zealand, commented that she was "noticeable as being the fourth of a very handy and handsome class of barques now in these waters, which have been built by Mr. Francis Robertson, Peterhead, the others being the clippers *Leonidas*, *Charlotte Andrews*, and *Prospector*. Under the heading PETERHEAD SHIPS AT THE ANTIPODES, the *Sentinel* relayed the news, on 27th January, 1865, as it might "be interesting to many readers in Peterhead." The *Southland* had made a passage of one hundred and one days to Invercargill, "the winds during the greater part of the time being very light and unfavourable but in all weathers she made very fine runs each day, passing several well-known fast sailing ships." The *Southland* returned to Britain and, on 19th July, 1865, was in London preparing to sail for the Cape of Good Hope.

The *Sentinel* was equally ready to cater for the interests of its readers when, on 25th October, 1867, it quoted the *Cape Advertiser* : "Among vessels at present at anchor in the Bay, is one which has made some of the quickest passages for some time past. We congratulate her owners for the admirable way in which she has been worked and we must not at the same time omit to give the credit due to Captain Thom for the manner in which he has managed his vessel. The *Southland* cleared from this port on 2nd March last for Guam and arrived at Valparaiso on 6th May. She there loaded a cargo of breadstuffs and left on 1st June. Her passage from Cape Horn was made in nineteen days and she arrived in Table Bay on 10th July. Her passage from this port was eastward and she has thus accomplished her voyage round the world, including stoppage, in four months and seven days. Amongst her previous passages were one from Table Bay to New York and back in three months and thirteen days and her last run from Algoa Bay to London in forty-five days. We have no doubt from the above that this fine vessel will meet immediate employment."

Universally recognised as a builder of top class vessels, Francis Robertson was contracted to build a 287-ton barque for the Arrow Line, trading between the Clyde and Natal. The *Ayr* was launched in January, 1865, and, when she left Peterhead in April, the *Sentinel* waxed lyrical about the vessel. "When we call the *Ayr* a fine vessel, we mean what we say. She is a fine model of a ship, she promises well for speed; and we have no doubt in the hands of so experienced an officer as Captain McEwan she will soon give a good account of herself and do credit to her builder and to Peterhead. Outside, the vessel looks well; but it is inside we must look to see what can be done locally in first-class work. The fittings of the saloon and ladies' cabin are really magnificent. The saloon is all side-panelled with walnut and bird eye maple - the roof being enamelled white, edged with gold, above the berth ventilators which are green. With a light Brussels carpet on the floor, the effect of the whole is very pretty. The saloon is fitted with berths for ten passengers and at one end (fixed in the partition of the ladies' cabin) is a fine register grate, with hearthstone and all appointments complete; in fact one at first imagines on looking around him that he is in the comfortable and elegant dining-room of a gentleman's mansion instead of being on board ship. In the ladies' cabin (which is fitted up in the same manner as the saloon, with walnut sofas, mirrors, etc.) there is accommodation for eight passengers, and in the second cabin (on deck) are the state rooms of the officers of the ship and accommodation for twelve passengers. From the fact that everything is so neatly, tastefully, and comfortably arranged on board, we cannot doubt that the *Ayr* will speedily become a favourite ship amongst the Arrow Line of packets between the Clyde and Natal."

Two years after leaving Peterhead, the *Ayr* was the subject of "a case of a rather peculiar nature which came under the notice of Sheriff Skelton." Peterhead Harbour Trustees and the owners of the vessel were at loggerheads regarding the period during which the vessel was being fitted out after being launched. The Trustees claimed that the *Ayr*, "was built near Port Henry and brought into harbour for repairs or completion and enjoyed the privilege of the protection of the harbours." They claimed that she was on a voyage from Peterhead to Glasgow at the time. The defenders held that the vessel was not on a voyage but in harbour to be completed. Giving his verdict, on 23rd April, 1867, the Sheriff began by quoting the regulations governing harbour dues : "For all vessels belonging to any part of Great Britain or Ireland when on a voyage to or from any port in Great Britain or Ireland, entering the harbours of Peterhead for safety or convenience, per register ton 3d. (less than 1½p)". He continued, "Now the vessel in question, which was not launched into the harbours of Peterhead, but from a private building yard in its close vicinity, and towed into one of the harbours by a rope or ropes, cannot be taken as entering the harbours of Peterhead when on a voyage..... (and she was not fitted for a voyage of any kind, being neither manned, rigged, provisioned, nor completed as a vessel), then the schedule does not apply to the situation at all."

Francis Robertson built two more vessels for the Arrow Line. In April, 1866, he launched the *Stinchar* which measured 150 feet overall and 393 tons N.M./480 tons builder's measurement. "A launch at Peterhead is quite a gala occasion," wrote a reporter in one of the *Sentinel's* periodic purple passages, "All who can get make up their minds that they must see it; and if any forgetful individual is seen "walking his pins" in another direction he runs the chance of being hailed by perhaps a hundred voices with - "Aren't ye gaen to see the launch?" He at last succumbs .... Every other inhabitant is there before him. The old lady has laid down her morning paper, the young lady her crochet, the maid-of-all-work her mop, the merchant has shut "for the nonce" his ledger, the clerk has laid down his quill, the tradesman has doffed his apron - and our very deevils (printer's devils) have laid down their sticks (to our horror, as we are just waiting on a proof) and all are off to the launch..... The vessel as we viewed her from our elevated position, had a fine appearance with her fine display of bunting..... The *Stinchar!* we are somewhat tickled by the name. We do not think it has a very euphonious sound; but we at last remember having heard of a small river of that name in Ayrshire and at once associate the one with the other. But our wandering senses are recalled - the carpenters have commenced knocking away the supports of the vessel; and in another minute she is off down those slippery ways and enters the water like a duck, the check-ropes only restraining her. A hearty cheer from those on deck is as heartily taken up by those on shore." In common with other Arrow Line boats, the *Stinchar* was registered in Ayr. She left Peterhead, on 19th May, to load coal at Shields for the East Indies and, a month later, a "launch ball, in connection with the *Stinchar*" was held in the Pavilion Hall, Broad Place.

When the *Inverary*, the last of the vessels built by Francis Robertson for the Arrow Line, was launched on 18th June, 1867, the *Sentinel* described "a scene at our harbours, the like of which had not occurred for the past 41 years"; two boats were launched on the same day from different yards. Watched by spectators on the North Pier, the *Inverary*, "a fine looking barque built under special survey and classed 8 years A1 at Lloyd's," went "gliding slowly and safely into her future element" and was followed soon after by the *Garron* from the yard of Stephen and Forbes. The *Inverary* left Peterhead on 18th July, 1867, bound for Leith to load general cargo for Adelaide.

The Coasting Trade

Most of the small merchant vessels built in Peterhead were destined for the North Sea coasting trade. Some, regularly plying particular routes, came to be identified as the recognised carriers of general cargo between Peterhead and a specified port; others shipped a wide variety of merchandise to and from harbours around the British coast. Especially in the years before the railway reached Peterhead, the bulk transport of goods, to and from the town, was almost entirely dependent on these craft, the unglamorous work-horses of the local mercantile fleet. As the contemporaneous accounts show, several fell victims to the vagaries of North Sea weather but others seemed to be endowed with an almost pheonix-like ability to survive extremely adverse conditions.

On 5th February, 1858, the *Sentinel* reported that "The *Hero*, Captain Huxtable, of this port, arrived in our bay on Sunday on her way from Leith with provisions for the Greenland vessels. Owing to a strong gale, she was unable to take the harbour and went south in the hope of finding refuge in Aberdeen, after having taken a pilot on board. Reaching Aberdeen about twelve o' clock on Sunday night, in attempting to take the harbour, the wind veered considerably and the vessel struck on the breakwater on the south side of the entrance. "Fortunately," says the *Aberdeen Journal*, "the casualty was observed by the Assistant-Captain Pilot and the watchman, who communicated with Mr. Guild, Captain Pilot." The seamen on board the *Hero* give a different statement and maintain that the pilots ought to have been at their aid at least an hour earlier than they were. The lights were up a considerable time before they struck on the rock. However, by means of *Manby's Life-Saving Apparatus*, after great exertions, all on board were safely brought on shore - five in number, including the pilot - and were well treated, Captain Robertson of the *Margaret and Jane* having considerably given them a number of dry clothes. To Mr. Robertson, Mr. Walker, innkeeper Torry, and others who lent their assistance, the highest praise is due. The vessel soon became a total wreck and the whole of the cargo is lost. Neither vessel nor cargo, we believe, were insured, so that the loss will fall heavily on those who were the owners, or had goods on board - we have heard the aggregate stated at £1,500, and the town will, of course, be that much poorer."

Carnegie and Matthew launched the 30-ton *Swift* for the Leith trade in August, 1859. Four months later, the *Sentinel*, quoting *The Scotsman*, gave "the unwelcome intelligence of the wreck of this vessel. The schooner, *Swift*, a regular trader between Peterhead and Leith was, during a severe storm on Saturday morning, and while on a voyage to the latter port, driven on shore on the south side of St. Andrews Bay, about fifteen miles east from the city. It was quite dark at the time (seven a.m.) and it was only after much difficulty that the crew succeeded in reaching the beach safely. The cargo on this occasion was principally composed of herring in barrels. The vessel has become a total wreck."

Less than four years later, on 20th February, 1863, one of the vessels which had been built fifteen years earlier for the Peterhead and London Shipping Company was the subject of the following report in the *Sentinel* : "We regret having to record this week the occurrence of a severe accident to the *Vivid* of this port - an accident which all but ended in the vessel becoming a total wreck. On Saturday evening, while on a voyage from Peterhead to London, (from what cause it is impossible to ascertain) she struck on the rocks in St. Cyrus Bay, about one and a half miles eastward from the parish church of St. Cyrus and quite close to the shore. "The crew," we are informed by the *Dundee Advertiser*, "took to the boat a short time after she struck, and, not knowing their whereabouts, sailed northwards until they reached Gourdon, the darkness of the night and the heavy sea preventing them from landing sooner. On Sunday morning, the men of the Coastguard stationed at Johnshaven boarded the vessel and a short time afterwards the crew returned and steps were taken at once to unload the stranded vessel." Most of the cargo - which though not heavy was valuable - comprising whalebone, sealskins, oatmeal etc. was saved although some of it was rather in a damaged state. We are glad, however, to record that on Tuesday forenoon the vessel was floated off the rocks and towed into Montrose harbour. The injuries she sustained are rather severe, the loss of the keel, the rudder etc." The *Vivid* was completely repaired and, after another five years' service with the Peterhead and London Shipping Company, was sold for £160 and towed to Aberdeen by the steam tug *Britannia*.

Another of the Peterhead and London Shipping Company's vessels, the 107-ton *Rapid*, built in the yard at Brook Lane in 1849, had a somewhat chequered career. Her passage from London to Peterhead in sixty hours in the first week in February, 1859, was described as "a remarkable instance of a quick passage in a sailing vessel." No longer employed only in the coasting trade, the *Rapid* was on a voyage from Shields to Oporto in April, 1868, when she had to "put into Grimsby with bows stove and loss of jib-boom, cutwater, figurehead, etc. having been in collision with a fishing smack" about twenty miles north east of Flamborough Head. In March the following year, she was towed into Dover, a derelict, after running ashore in the East Bay of Dungeness while on a voyage from Poole to London with a cargo of pipe-clay. Her mate died of cholera in Königsberg

in August, 1873, and when the *Rapid* arrived in Peterhead Bay, "it was, of course, necessary to use all medical precautions. Dr. Jamieson, medical officer for the local authority, made careful inspection of the vessel and, having pronounced her free from infectious diseases, she was permitted to enter the harbour." Her entry in the *Register of Shipping* was closed on 22nd January, 1877, after she was wrecked at Kinnaird Head.

The *Mermaid*, described as a 72-ton schooner with an eliptic stern, sharp bow, and clipper rig, was launched by Carnegie and Matthew, on 12th September, 1872, for a firm based in Newburgh, Aberdeenshire. The builders were "careful to construct her upon a principle which makes her most suitable for trading to Newburgh, lightness of draught being a considerable recommendation."

Other vessels built in Peterhead for the coasting trade were bought by ship-owners outwith the town. For example, the 52-ton *Volunteer* went to Dublin in 1860; the 45-ton *Hawk* was transferred to Berwick in 1863; the 56-ton *Onward* was built for a Dublin owner in 1865; the 41-ton *Conquest* was bought by a Fraserburgh sea-captain in 1867; and the 108-ton *Viking* was built for a customer in Wick in 1873. The 74-ton *C. S. Parnell*, "with a figurehead of a bust of Mr. Parnell, M.P., with a roll in his right hand against his breast", was built in 1882 for the ship-owner who had bought the *Onward* seventeen years previously.

In February, 1872, the *Sentinel* chronicled the loss of a former Leith trader. "On Thursday last, the *Active*, Capt. Sutherland, went on the rocks near the South Head and has since become a total wreck. She had come into harbour but a few days previously and, having discharged fifty tons of guano, was on her way to Nairn with the remainder. Heavy sea and the state of the wind and tide drove her on shore. Coastguardsmen soon had the crew ashore. A number of hands working during the night landed a considerable portion of the cargo. .... The hull of the vessel was sold on Monday to George Milne, Roanheads, for £18.5s. (£18.25) The other materials fetched rather good prices." When wrecked, the *Active*, which had been built in 1851 by Scott and Stevenson on Keith Inch, was registered in Sunderland. She had been "in the news" in March, 1865, under the heading, "A WELL-MERITED GIFT", when readers of the *Sentinel* learned that "On Wednesday, Captain Fraser of the *Active* was presented with nine pounds and his crew with fourteen pounds five shillings (£14.25) by a few of the merchants and shippers of Peterhead - principally by those who had goods on board the tight little vessel when she so bravely rode out the late tremendous storm."

When, after sixteen years in the Leith trade, the vessel was bought, in March, 1867, by a Fraserburgh fishcurer for £355, the *Sentinel* hastened to re-assure its readers, "As will be seen from our advertisement columns, the public are not to suffer long for want of a Leith trader, Mr. Alex. Bruce having at once made arrangements to ply his smack *Helen* twixt here and Leith. She is expected to leave today." The relevant advertisement announced, "The smack, *Helen*, Captain Alex. Bruce, is at present in the harbour taking GOODS for Leith and will be clear to sail on Friday (today) 22nd March. The *Helen* will return from Leith with goods for Peterhead. By charging moderate freights, Alexander Bruce hopes to merit the public's patronage. The *Helen* will not carry Naphtha or Paraffin."

When a new boat was built for Alex. Bruce, the *Sentinel*, in reporting the launch, took the opportunity to extol one of the cardinal virtues of the Victorian era, self-improvement by self-help. On 16th November, 1870, readers learned that "Yesterday afternoon there was launched from the building yard of Stephen and Forbes, a handsome clipper schooner, which is to take the place of the *Fairy* on the passage between Peterhead and Leith. The vessel was named *Nelly* and the ceremony was performed by Mrs.Bruce, wife of Captain Bruce, who is both master and owner. The *Nelly* is 65 feet (under 20 metres) of keel; 8 feet 4 inches (about 2.5 metres) hold; and 19 feet (less than 6 metres) beam. She is 68 tons N.M. and is copper-bottomed, copper-fastened, and is, both in respect of model and workmanship, in every way worthy of her builders. We have no doubt that the public will show their appreciation of the energy and enterprise of Captain Bruce in placing such a fine vessel on the passage by patronising him even more liberally than hithertofore. Captain Bruce began the coasting trade with only a herring boat, and by his enterprise and care, he has risen by degrees till he is now master of the admirable schooner launched yesterday. The *Nelly* was much admired by onlookers and at once recognised as a worthy addition to the many fine vessels turned out by Stephen and Forbes."

When the *Nelly* left Peterhead on her maiden voyage in November, 1870, "she tacked for a while in the Bay but, owing to the light wind, her sailing capacities could not be properly tested. At any rate, she looked well. A strong breeze from the southward setting in some time afterwards compelled Captain Bruce to put into Aberdeen harbour." Three months later, the *Sentinel* reported, "The new clipper schooner *Nelly*, Capt. Bruce, returned to harbour on Saturday morning with her foremast broken. The vessel left for Leith on Friday forenoon and early on Saturday morning, when some fifteen miles off Slains Castle, and when it blew fresh from about S.S.E., the foremast gave way close at the head. The crew

succeeded in clearing and making fast the loose gear; and a few hours after, no other damage having been sustained, the *Nelly* ran into harbour. The broken mast was replaced by a new one and the vessel is now ready for sea again." On another occasion, in 1872, while moored in harbour, she broke adrift during a gale, "damaged the *Enterprise's* stern, and broke her own headgear."

After being withdrawn from the Leith trade, she continued to operate as a coaster, being severely damaged in a storm in October, 1877, and again in November, 1881. On the latter occasion, the local press reported, "In the course of the gale on Thursday, the schooner *Nelly* of Peterhead was in a somewhat dangerous position off St Andrews. Signals were shown for a pilot but owing to the roughness of the sea it was impracticable for one to go out. By a fortunate circumstance, the old lifeboat stationed at Boarhills was being brought by sea to St Andrews and several of her crew went aboard the *Nelly*. The vessel then attempted the harbour and although she struck three times, she was got into the harbour safely." She was made seaworthy once again and, in December, 1882, was transferred to the *Belfast Register*.

The *Nelly* was replaced in the Leith trade in 1873 by the *Sweet Home* (*J11* on page 105), a smack of 30 tons, which had been employed as a coaster since her launch from Florence's yard in May, 1868. The *Sweet Home* continued as a Leith trader until she was replaced by the *Welcome Home* (*J12* on page 105).

After being launched from the yard of Stephen and Forbes in November, 1885, the *Welcome Home* was described in the *Buchan Observer* as copper-bottomed and purpose-built for the Leith trade. With copper fastenings and "air-tight bulkheads in isolated parts of the vessel where paraffin and other obnoxious goods may be stored and thus not affect the general cargo", she was said to be "capitally adapted for the purpose." She was sold furth of Peterhead after nearly eight years in the Leith trade and became a total loss in August, 1900, when she was stranded on the North Pier, Aberdeen, while bound for Little Ferry with a cargo of lime from Sunderland.

A second *Sweet Home* (*J13* on page 106) took the place of the *Welcome Home* as a Leith trader in 1893. It was a sign of the times that she was a steamer built in Bowling and that another steamer built furth of Peterhead, the *Susu* (*J14* on page 106), became a regular on the Leith run before Edward VII was crowned. As the country's mercantile marine became increasingly composed of steam-driven, steel-built vessels, the once burgeoning ship-building industry in Peterhead almost disappeared, with the surviving yards concentrating on producing fishing boats.

J11 The Sweet Home entering the South Harbour, Peterhead.

J12 The Welcome Home in the South Harbour; Harbour Street on the left; Cormack's Slip beyond the bow.

J13 *The s.s. Sweet Home leaving the South Harbour, Peterhead.*

J14 *The s.s. Susu entering the South Harbour. Fares to Aberdeen - one shilling and sixpence (7½ p) steerage,*
two shillings (10p) cabin; to Leith - five shillings (25p) steerage, seven shillings and sixpence (37½ p) cabin.
The company reserved the right to run special trips to Leith with herrings, as required, on Mondays.

THE VOLUNTEER MOVEMENT

At a meeting of Peterhead Town Council on 10th June, 1859, one of the Bailies, eloquent in support of what he called "one of the most important movements which has taken place for years", outlined the factors which had led the Government to recommend the establishment of a national network of local Volunteer Corps. "Europe," he said, "is at present in an agitated state; some of the leading powers are now actually at war and others, as well as ourselves, are setting armies and navies in order." He argued that although Britain had publicly declared its neutrality in the current disputes between France, Sardinia, and Austria, this was no justification for complacency. As he pointed out, most of our army was in "our Eastern dominions" where the campaign to suppress the Indian Mutiny had ended only months previously. His proposal that the Provost should convene an early meeting of the inhabitants of the town "to consider the propriety of forming Volunteer Artillery and Rifle Corps in this district of Aberdeenshire" was greeted with cheers. The Provost, however, argued that there was no need for such haste. He thought that if, as had been suggested, Peterhead became a naval base, the Government might erect forts and so they could have an Artillery Corps. After being reminded that the Government had paid all the expenses of the volunteer corps in Peterhead during the Napoleonic Wars, the canny councillors decided to postpone convening a public meeting until more details of the Government's intentions regarding the new Volunteer Corps were available.

Five weeks later, the *Peterhead Sentinel* reported that more than 150 inhabitants had united in requesting the Provost to call a public meeting. By then, the Government had agreed to provide 25 rifles for every 100 men who enrolled in a Rifle Corps and participated in the recommended drill; rifles for the others had to be financed locally and members were expected to pay for their own uniforms. In the editor's opinion, the Government should have undertaken to provide all the rifles and should also have removed the restriction that Rifle Corps should have practice grounds extending to at least a clear range of 300 yards. He also reminded his readers that "At one time, we had a battery at this port and the guns were removed, we believe, under the express condition of being replaced whenever occasion required. Now is the time."

By the time a public meeting was held on 5th August, 1859, the Government had informed the Lords Lieutenant in maritime counties of the desirability of forming Artillery Corps rather than Rifle Corps and that, if this was done, guns would be provided for training and practice. It was decided to appoint a committee to discuss the formation of Corps of Volunteers and to draft rules and regulations for them.

The committee proposed the formation of a Corps of Artillery Volunteers and a Corps of Rifle Volunteers but recommended that the former should receive special encouragement. Although both Corps had to conform in all respects to Government regulations, the committee drafted the "Standing Orders" for the local management of the Volunteers. A Committee of ten members was to be elected annually, with four members being returned from the old to the new Committee without elections. Committee meetings were to be held on the first Monday of each month and a Secretary and a Treasurer would enrol members and manage the affairs of each Corps. Volunteers had to pay for their own uniforms and any accoutrements not supplied by the Government. Each Corps was to consist of two classes of members, effective and non-effective; while each class would have a voice in the disposal of funds, only the effectives were to be allowed to recommend members to the Lord Lieutenant for appointment as officers. To enable the Volunteers to identify "potential officer material", there were to be at least two months' drills before the first recommendations were made. Each effective member had to contribute 10s.6d (52½p) annually to the funds of the Rifle Corps or 5s.3d (26½p) annually to the funds of the Artillery Corps; each non-effective had to contribute 21 shillings (£1.05) to the Rifle Corps or 10s.6d (52½p) to the Artillery Corps. The first subscription was to be paid on enrolment and no one would be considered a member whose annual subscription was in arrear for more than two months. Retirement would be permitted on seven days' notice but all arrears had to be paid before retirement. Absentees from a prescribed drill would be fined unless a written excuse was given. In order to defray the expenses incurred during the formation of the Corps, subscription lists were opened immediately. For contributions of £2.12s.6d (£2.62½) to the Artillery Corps, or five guineas (£5.25) to the Rifle Corps, the donors would become life members of the corps to which the donations were made.

The progress of the Volunteer Movement, nationally as well as locally, continued to feature prominently in the columns of the *Peterhead Sentinel*. Appeals were made to the patriotic spirit of the inhabitants and attention was drawn to recruiting successes in other areas with the implication that it was up to the inhabitants of Peterhead to do just as well, if not better. In spite of this, recruitment was slow at first because of the financial implications of enrolling; in addition to the cost of uniform and equipment, volunteers risked losing wages if they required time off work to attend the drills.

The Corps of Artillery Volunteers at Peterhead

By mid-December, 100 artillerymen had enrolled and the Lord Lieutenant, the Earl of Aberdeen, requested the Secretary of State for War to sanction the formal establishment of a Corps of Artillery Volunteers at Peterhead. The editor of the *Sentinel* predicted, "We may expect to see our outlying promontory well armed with heavy guns manned by the flower of our town, able and willing to give a good account of every shot they may send towards a hostile cruiser. We believe those volunteers will be enrolled solely for the purpose of working heavy guns placed in batteries for the defence of the harbours and bays of Peterhead and will not be moveable in case of war." The editor's highlighting of the exclusively local nature of the Volunteers' patriotic commitments may have been designed to encourage further recruitment but many of his readers will have been more impressed by his comment that "as the Government provides guns and ammunition, the Corps will be put to very little expense for equipment."

At the end of December, 1859, the Secretary of State for War answered the Earl of Aberdeen : "I have the honour to acknowledge receipt of your lordship's letter of 14th instant, offering for the Queen's acceptance the service of a Corps of Artillery Volunteers at Peterhead under the Act 44 Geo 3c 54 and to inform you in reply that Her Majesty has been graciously pleased to approve and accept the same. The maximum establishment of the corps will consist of :- Captain Commandant; Captain; 2 First Lieutenants; 2 Second Lieutenants; 160 men of all ranks divided into two companies. I have further to inform your lordship that the county of Aberdeen holds the 32nd place in the Artillery Volunteer Force of Great Britain and that this corps is the first in Aberdeenshire. Signed S. Herbert."

Eight weeks later, the Artillery Volunteers met in Peterhead Academy (*K1* below) to elect their officers. The resultant appointments in the First Company were: Captain Commandant - Mr. Hutchison of Monyruy; First Lieutenant - James Morrison, Accountant; Second Lieutenant - Patrick Jamieson, Surgeon. In the Second Company, the appointees were : Captain - Mr. Arbuthnot of Invernettie; First Lieutenant - David Gray, Shipmaster; Second Lieutenant - P. Irvine, Solicitor. It was also agreed that the Committee should "make arrangements for drill and settling the style of the uniform, which will probably be that recommended by the government, specimen coloured drawings of which have now been received." A tunic, trousers, and forage cap, with

K1 Peterhead Academy was founded, in 1838, as an independent school for boys in a single-storey building at the corner of St. Peter Street and Prince Street. After the Academy was re-located on its current site (See C6), the original building was heightened and used as the Central School.

waist and shoulder belts, ball bag, cap pocket, gaiters, knee caps, and bayonet trog, cost approximately £3.4s. (£3.20); a great coat, which was not regarded as essential, cost at least another £1.10s. (£1.50).

On Monday, 2nd April, 1860, drill commenced under the instruction of Sgt. Neal who, posted from the Royal Artillery personnel in Leith Fort, had arrived in Peterhead the previous week. The *Sentinel* reported that there were four sessions during the day with 20 to 50 attending on each occasion. In the same issue, readers learned that the foundation stone had been laid for the Torry Battery, which was being built for the Aberdeen Artillery Volunteers. They were also told that twenty to thirty good builders would find immediate employment at good wages and "that the work is so far progressed as to ensure the masons full time."

The Peterhead Batteries were not built as expeditiously. Three suitable sites had been identified for the guns. The editor of the *Sentinel* commented, "The first requirement is the ground and this rests with the Hospital"; i.e. the Governors of the Merchant Maiden Hospital in Edinburgh, the Superiors of the town. "The Town Council and the community have done their part," he continued, "let the Governors do theirs with equal promptitude."

In a letter dated 18th April, 1860, the Governors' Factor in Peterhead informed the Town Council, "The Governors will give, at nominal charge, two sites on Keith Inch containing one sixth and one third of an acre. Provision must be made for preserving entire the road or "pleasure walk" marked on the plan around Keith Inch. It is understood that the site extending to one sixth of an acre is that which the former battery occupied and the other is the rocky ground lying eastward of the road above referred to. With regard to the site at Roanheads, the Governors will give it on payment of the value of the houses upon it and at 47s.6d (£2.37½) per pole (30.25 square yards or 25.3 square metres)." In his next issue, the editor of the *Sentinel* published a scathing attack on the Governors of the Merchant Maiden Hospital, accusing them of putting an exorbitant price on the ground required for the battery at Roanheads. "£380 per acre," he fulminated, "for land on which nobody but a fisherman would build at a rent of £4 annually. With regard to the present battery, which the Governors make a virtue of presenting to the Government at a nominal feu duty, more than 200 years ago the Feuars erected it and townspeople manned it when occasion required; in the beginning of this century, the Feuars re-built it and again did good service with it. Doubtless the Governors thought their generosity at the South Harbour would cancel their avarice at the North. The Governors make excellent volunteers and patriot in Edinburgh

but they are about the opposite in Peterhead."

Despite the frustration of the impasse in the negotiations regarding the erection of the batteries and although doubts were still being expressed about men being able to afford the expense of membership of the Corps, most of the artillerymen were "in uniform" before the end of June, 1860. "On Wednesday and Saturday, they proceed to the links and it is pleasant to see the accuracy and promptitude with which they go through their evolutions. The dress is rich and becoming," the *Sentinel* reported, "all we now require is the batteries!"

By mid-July, the first consignment of guns - two 32 pounders with carriages and all the requisite mountings - were landed on the South Pier from the Leith trader, *Active*. As may be imagined, they were "an object of interest and wonder to the inhabitants." Sgt. Neal spent the day making arrangements for their removal to the old battery on the Keith Inch. In the evening, the Corps assembled in uniform to drag them to the battery and "did so in excellent style preceded by the band, whose performances led by Drum-Major Coombs were greatly appreciated by the immense concourse of people assembled to witness this rare and interesting spectacle." This must have been the first public performance of the Artillery Corps Band. Although the instruments - bass drum, two brass side drums, eight fifes and triangles - had been delivered early in June, Sgt. Drum-Major Coombs of the Royal Aberdeenshire Highlanders had not arrived until the first week in July to take up the post of band-master. Another consignment of two 32 pounders arrived by sea during the first week in August and, as on the previous occasion, were dragged into position alongside the others. The *Sentinel* commented, somewhat superfluously, "Mounted on their carriages, they (the guns) had really a formidable and military-like appearance"!

K2 Artillery Volunteers on Keith Inch, in 1860.

The Corps then met to elect their Non-Commissioned Officers. Alex. Forbes, shipbuilder; M. Beveridge, Comptroller of Customs; C. Nicol, printer; and J.H. Will, fishcurer, were chosen as Sergeants. John Loggie was appointed Drum-Major, while Alex. Brown, draper; Alex. McDonald, flesher; R. Sutherland, flesher; and A. Morrison of the London and Leith Shipping Co. became Corporals. The Bombardiers were Wm. Leslie, fishcurer; Alex. Ingram, fishcurer; J. Henderson, painter; and E. Allan, writer.

Soon afterwards, the Volunteers received some welcome free publicity. In reporting a launch from the yard of Messrs Stephen and Forbes, the *Sentinel* enthused, "The builders deserve credit for the taste and tact they evince in always "hitting the current" so admirably in their selection of names." The vessel, soon to be sold to a Dublin shipowner, was built "on spec" and so the name, *Volunteer*, was presumably the choice of one of the partners, Alex. Forbes, who had recently been appointed a Sergeant in the Artillery Corps. During the launch, the cable was cut by an Artillery Volunteer and a Rifle Volunteer in full uniform. The band of the Artillery Corps was on board and, "as she glided gracefully into the water, they played a stirring and appropriate air."

The Band Funds benefited by over £17 when a *Grand Military Concert* was held on Friday, 31st August, 1860, in Mr. Nicol's Hall, 18 Jamaica Street. The Band, during its first concert performance in uniform, contributed items to the programme of vocal and instrumental music. The Artillery Volunteers in the audience were in uniform and added to the spectacle of the occasion when "Over the platform was erected a spacious arch of evergreens tastefully variegated with flowers. Similar arches adorned the walls, besides banners, and stars ingeniously formed of swords, pistols, bayonets, carbines, etc."

The Corps mustered near the Academy at 4.30 p.m. on Saturday, 1st September, 1860, for their first Review. After inspecting both companies and witnessing their "evolutions" during a continuous downpour, Colonel Fraser, the Vice Lord Lieutenant of Aberdeenshire, said he was highly satisfied. In the following week, after being inspected by Lieutenant Blades, Inspector of Artillery for the North East Coast of Scotland, the corps was told that it was the best he had seen! A month later, a Colonel and a Lieutenant of the Royal Artillery visited to take measurements preparatory to the erection of the batteries. Arrangements were made for drill, in the Company shed in Lodge Walk, with the carbines and bayonets which had been delivered recently, and efforts were made to enrol a further 20-25 members who had to be willing to contribute part, at least, of the cost of their own uniforms.

The Secretary of State for War announced two schemes designed to encourage recruitment of Artillery Volunteers and Rifle Volunteers. In addition to a plan to "enable artizans and others to obtain their uniform and necessary equipment", a National Volunteer Mutual Association was planned to provide medical attendance, a weekly allowance during sickness, age-related pensions, and a sum payable on death.

At the end of November, 1860, the Volunteers were inspected by the Adjutant of the newly formed Brigade which consisted of the Aberdeenshire Companies, among which the Peterhead Corps was designated "First". One of the guns had been moved to the Company shed for exercise during the winter months and so the Volunteers were told off in gun-detachments for the three guns still on Keith Inch. They could not fire even blank cartridges, however, as the guns had not been proved by a Government surveyor! Nevertheless, members were issued with their "required reading" - lithographed sheets entitled *Instructions for Preparing Common and Diaphragm Fuzes* and *Instructions for Loading, Scouring, and Preparing Common and Diaphragm Shells for Firing.*

Eventually, on 12th January, 1861, fully eighteen months after the formation of an Artillery Corps was first mooted, watched by numerous spectators, the first practice rounds - 25 in all - were fired from the guns on Keith Inch at targets positioned 1,300 yards (1.188 km) out in the bay. The next practice session, at the beginning of February, also attracted a large number of spectators. Targets were placed at 1,765 (1.614 km) and 1,325 (1.211 km) yards and 68 rounds were fired. Results were generally good but the platform of the eastmost gun was reported to be in a bad condition. In the following months, the Corps met frequently for gun practice with satisfactory results in spite of the effect of wind and wave on the targets moored at varying distances in the bay; on one occasion one of the shots knocked down the flagstaff on the target!

With the Corps now fully operational as regards weaponry - guns and carbines - contracts were placed at the beginning of May, 1861, for the supply of cross belts and cartouch boxes for holding cartridges. When they were issued in July, the uniform of the Artillery Volunteers was complete.

In a further attempt to keep the expenses of Volunteers to a minimum, the Government introduced the Volunteer Toll Exemption Bill in May, 1861. Volunteers, in uniform, were exempted from tolls, pier dues, or pontages when travelling in connection with their duties. Similar exemption was given to horses, carriages, etc. employed in conveying the arms and baggage of Volunteers. Anyone falsely presenting himself as a Volunteer to evade tolls was subject to a penalty, not exceeding £5, as was any toll keeper who demanded tolls from a Volunteer.

The Volunteers began to play a significant role in the social and cultural life of the community. In April, 1861, assisted by Miss Mortimer, of the Theatre Royal, Edinburgh, and Miss Wilson, of the Theatre Royal, Dundee, they presented a GRAND ARTILLERY VOLUNTEER THEATRICAL ENTERTAINMENT in Broad Place Pavilion as a result of which £15 was added to the funds of the Corps. The *Sentinel* drew a veil over the performances of the visiting artistes with the terse comment, "Of the actresses, Misses Wilson and Mortimer, perhaps (although we do not wish at all to appear ungallant) the less said the better." On the other hand, the performances of the men met with general acclaim and, having experienced the smell of the grease paint, they resolved to form a Dramatic Club.

The new club's first productions were advertised on 27th December, 1861: "GRAND THEATRICAL PERFORMANCES in aid of the funds of the 1st Aberdeenshire Artillery Volunteers. Peterhead Dramatic Corps, assisted by Miss Regina Brooke (late of the Theatre Royal, Leicester) and Miss Harriet Crossman (late of the Princess Theatre and Tully's Opera Company, London) will give a series of Dramatic performances in the Concert Room, Jamaica Street, commencing on the evening of Tuesday, 31st December, with the beautiful Melo-dramatic Play of *DON CAEZAR DE BAZAN* or *A Match for the King*. To conclude with the laughable Extravaganza entitled *THE BONNIE FISHWIFE*.
Boxes 2s. (10p); Pit 1s.; (5p); Gallery 6d (2½) Doors open at half past seven. Curtain to rise at eight o'clock."

In spite of the incongruous double bill, the *Sentinel* reported favourably on this performance in which "The ladies were a vast improvement upon those of last year." Commenting on the venue, it said, "The Room is rather small to afford space for stage, boxes, pit, and gallery, not to mention the orchestra; but although everything is in miniature, arrangements for the accommodation of both players and audience are admirably carried out, with one slight exception - there might be considerable improvements on the boxes." The "season" continued for three weeks during which the number and variety of productions, catering for all tastes, would have done credit to a professional repertory company. The "Grand National Drama of *Rob Roy*! or *Auld Lang Syne*, with all the songs and choruses and improved Scenic Effect and Stage Paraphernalia", was performed on

the same evening as Kenny's laughable farce of *Raising The Wind*. Shakespeare's *Othello*, which was "performed in a very creditable manner", shared the bill with the "farce of *The Rough Diamond*, which was a hit and kept the audience in roars of laughter." Another marathon programme consisted of *The Merchant of Venice* and a popular farce, *The Boots at The Inn*. *The Black Eyed Susan*, *Gilderoy*, and *Good For Nothing* were also included in the repertoire.

As well as performing its primary duty - leading the Volunteers "on parade" - the Artillery Band was called upon periodically to provide an appropriately patriotic accompaniment when the occasion warranted this. When, for example, the schooner, *Bannockburn*, was launched in August, 1865, the band was on deck and "struck up the heart-stirring and truly national tune, *Scots Wha Hae*, as she dashed into the vasty deep." In the following April, the schooner, *Wallace*, was launched "in majestic style, amid the cheers of the numerous onlookers and the stirring music of the Volunteer Artillery brass band who, in their best style, played *Scots Wha Hae*, *Off She Goes*, *The Boatie Rows* etc."

These extraneous activities were, of course, incidental to the main activities of the Corps. Lieutenant Morrison, for example, lectured the Volunteers on *The Theoretical Principles of Rifle Shooting*! There was a weekly programme of Drill and Gun Practice, which was no longer confined to the one day stipulated in the original *Rules and Regulations*, and it was not uncommon for "exercises" to be held every evening in the weeks before the Annual Inspection.

The War Office increased the allowance of ammunition to every Artillery Volunteer Corps in January, 1862. Blank cartridges became almost redundant and, as each battery was given 100 rounds of shot and 25 shells, the gunnery sessions became more spectacular. During the Annual Inspection in October, 1862, "There was gun practice at the battery, from the 4 guns there, at a spar with a flag as target moored at 1,300 yards (1.188 km) and some beautiful ball practice was made although, among the spectators, there was more interest in the shell practice, which had a very fine effect as the dark of evening set in - most of the shells bursting right in front of or above the targets." The Inspecting Officer expressed his regret that a larger number had not turned out but promised that his next visit would be "at a period of the year more generally suited for the leisure of the members"!

In March, 1863, a mock-heroic poem, dedicated to the police commissioners and entitled *Sweet Peterhead*, appeared in the *Sentinel*. A parody of *The Isles of Greece* by Lord Byron, to whom neither apology nor acknowledgement was made, it had been submitted by "a sarcastic correspondent, who apparently has a better appreciation of the Volunteers than of our civic senators".

Sweet Peterhead! Sweet Peterhead!
Where many a Sophy loved and sung,
Where many a herring was smoked red,
And odours foul from blubber sprung;
Thy scent assails our nostrils yet,
Thy muddy streets are ever wet!

Delightful town where fogs and rains
Alternate oriental gales,
Which waft along thy streets and lanes
The incense of decaying whales,
Each muddy gutter witness bears
To inefficient scavengers!

The town looks down on Queenie's Isle,
And Queenie's Isle looks to the sea;
And there one day I mused a while,
Beside the frowning Battery;
Could sons of sires who dared the whale
Before the French barbarians quail.?

No! while one drop of blood remains
To warm their hearts with generous fire,
Proud victory shall crown their pains
Or for their country they expire;
Such were the men of Macedon,
And such the sons of Caledon!

Shortly afterwards, the gun platforms were re-laid and a store shed was built at the battery. The Feuars and the Harbour Trustees promised to meet the cost of removing the "unseemly and ruinous-looking embankment of earth outside the battery" and of building "a low wall with a coping which will form a convenient seat all round the outside of the work, from which the bay, ships, and herring boats can be conveniently surveyed." In welcoming these proposals, the *Sentinel* took the opportunity to continue the campaign for all the surrounding area on Keith Inch to be given a thorough face-lift. The Road Trustees or Commissioners of Police were exhorted to do something to have the roads put in a better state so that the "one which has the words *Pleasure Walk* so conspicuously painted up at the Guard House would become worthy of its name."

While the improvements to the Battery were being discussed, the guns were all declared to be in a serviceable condition after a Royal Artillery Major, accompanied by a small detachment of mechanics from the gun factory at Woolwich, carried out a minute inspection. Two months later, however, a sub-standard gun practice was attributed to the deficient state of the recently re-laid platforms. That this was not a case of bad workmen blaming their

tools was proved convincingly when the Peterhead contingent won the Heavy Gun Competition at the Aberdeenshire Volunteer Artillery and Rifle Association Annual Wapinschaw at the Broad Hill, Aberdeen, in July, 1863.

The Government now decided to introduce a scheme for the certification of Volunteers. On 1st December, each year, the Brigade Adjutant had to issue certificates of efficiency, valid for one year, to Volunteers who complied with stipulated requirements, some of which were specific to the type of Corps - Light Horse, Artillery, Engineer, Mounted Rifle, or Rifle. In all Corps, recruits had to serve a probationary period of eighteen months. Volunteers beyond the recruit stage had to attend the prescribed drills during the year and be on parade for the Annual Inspection when Inspecting Officers could withhold certificates from those they regarded as not sufficiently proficient. Volunteers who were refused certificates could appeal to the Commanding Officer and, if still not satisfied, to "higher authority". Rather incongruously, the Secretary of State had the power to give Artillery Volunteers dispensation from attendance at gun practice!

Competitive shooting for cash prizes was becoming increasingly common within the Volunteer movement, especially in the Rifle Corps. The Artillery Corps had not attracted any sponsorship and so the following advertisement appeared in the *Sentinel* in September, 1863. "GRAND ARTILLERY COMPETITION A few of the Rank and File of Peterhead Artillery, despairing of ever having a Prize offered them for Competition have resolved to shoot for some Prizes supplied by themselves. These will be: First - Swineyard Clay Cutty Pipe slightly damaged from the stalk having been accidentally broken but none the worse of that. Second - One half ounce Superior Irish Twist Tobacco. Third - One second hand Tin Snuffbox with Plate for Inscription, original value, 1½d (less than 1p). Fourth - One box very superior Patent Paraffin Congreves. Competition at the Range at Geddle Braes, on a day to be fixed hereafter. Conditions - 150, (about 137 metres) 200, (about 183 metres) and 300 yards (about 274 metres)- 24 shots at each. Competitors requested to furnish own ammunition." There is no record of the outcome of this advertisement but we may safely assume that, with a box of matches as the fourth prize, none of the Volunteers was taken in by the spoof!

The Annual Inspection in September, 1863, was reported fully in the *Sentinel*, "On the order, "Form fours, right", the company, preceded by their band, marched through the town to the Links and there awaited the arrival of the Inspector. In a short time, Colonel MacLean, Leith Fort, accompanied by

Colonel Gordon, superior officer of the Aberdeenshire Brigade (of which the Peterhead Companies are the 1st and 2nd) and Adjutant Kinnear, appeared on the ground and was received by a general salute, the band playing a stave of the *National Anthem*..... several infantry movements were executed fairly enough, although an occasional unsteadiness here and there betrayed a forgetfulness of their company drill by those who have not been sufficiently assiduous in their attendance on company practices...... Carbines were inspected and the Colonel was highly pleased with the state of the arms with the exception of one which, we understand, had been kept in the possession of the individual member contrary to orders. Next was "testing men at their own peculiar arm - the garrison guns". Arriving at the Armoury, carbines, sword-bayonets, and cross-belts were deposited there..... As this corps has twice borne away the Artillery medal at the Aberdeen Wapinschaw, the disappointment of the gunners may well be imagined when, on looking through the embrasures, they looked in vain for the targets on which to exhibit their skill. Targets were placed in the bay at a distance of 1,800 yards (1.646 km) but, as they consist simply of an upright spar with a flag on top of it, the strong breeze blowing and the heavy sea completely hid them from the naked eye; they could only be discerned by means of a glass, so there could be no ball practice." The Colonel, echoing the regrets expressed a year earlier, commented that he would have liked to have seen a larger muster than the 5 officers, 4 sergeants, and 64 rank and file on parade.

Co-incidentally, the following advertisement appeared in the edition which contained the above report! "JUST OUT: a TELESCOPE for £5 which will distinguish the face of a sheep and features of a man - four miles; the sign of a public house - five miles; *shot marks upon a target - two miles* (my italics); time by a church clock - ten miles; and the planets and double stars. Guaranteed in writing to perform the whole of the above and to be equal to a telescope costing £70. B.SOLOMON & CO. 39 Albemarle-Street, Piccadilly, London.W."

In May, 1865, when preparing for the Annual Inspection, the Corps was informed that it was to be supplied "with Busbys which will effect great improvement on the appearance of the Company" (*K3*). During the inspection, a direct hit was scored on the target - a flagstaff buoyed with cork 1,300 yards (1.188 km) out in the bay - causing the Inspecting Officer, a Colonel in the Royal Artillery, to enthuse, "You are perfect at gun drill. I am not in the habit of seeing gun drill done so well anywhere. I may say not even in the Royal Artillery." He complimented the officers "who appear to have learned and to know how to carry out their duties" but he chastised the "old hands", including the perfect

gunners, "It is obvious to me that you have not attended too well to company drill as your marching and wheeling were not so steady as they might have been"!

K3 *Artillery Volunteer officer photographed, in full dress, by Joseph Collier in 1865-66.*

As the training programme for the following summer indicates, those responsible for the proficiency of the Corps took steps to remedy this weakness before the next annual inspection. "Gun Drill at the Battery on Monday, Tuesday, Thursday at half past seven; Company Drill on Wednesday at 15 minutes before 8; Carbine Drill on Friday at half past seven; and Carbine Practice at the new range at the brickworks every Saturday afternoon at 4 o'clock. Ball Practice at the Battery throughout the summer." It is perhaps not surprising that, a week after the promulgation of these rather daunting *Routine Orders*, there was "a poor turn out" when Adjutant Kinnear met the Volunteers at the Armoury.

The performance of Volunteers parading for exercises and inspections continued to be of an acceptably high standard. Some, however, were no longer motivated by the novelty factor and, in addition to "natural wastage" and resignations, a significant number were habitually absent. By June, 1877, the number on parade for the Annual Inspection had dwindled to 57. In the following year, 65 Artillery Volunteers were inspected by Colonel Bolton, Commander of Reserve Forces of the North of Scotland. By 1882, the Corps numbered 70, of whom 60 - 2 officers, 5 sergeants, and 53 rank and file - were inspected by Colonel Kelly Holdsworth, Commandant of the North of Scotland, accompanied by Colonel Garden Campbell of Troup.

The proficiency of the gunners remained as high as ever. The lack of sponsorship, so satirically highlighted in 1863, had been overcome. A "handsome silver cup presented to the 1st Aberdeenshire Artillery Volunteers by the Governors of the Merchant Maiden Hospital was presented to Gunner Ogston" on 27th July, 1870. Some eight years later, when six detachments of gunners competed on Keith Inch for the cup presented by the Governors of the Merchant Maiden Hospital, each man in the winning detachment received 5 shillings (25p). In July, 1878, the *Sentinel* was pleased to report that "the handsome silver bugle, which was the first prize at Aberdeen Wapinschaw and was carried off by our local artillerymen against all comers, is presently on view in W. L. Taylor's window."

By this time, the Admiralty was negotiating for a site for a new Battery at the Roanheads. Once again, the price asked by the Superiors was considered to be too high. A less-than-subtle play on local rivalry - a suggestion that a Battery might be built at Fraserburgh - resulted in the offer of a site at Gadle Braes! The Admiralty accepted and, in November, 1881, there was a request for "stones for platforms for the New Battery from the dismantled Old Battery on Keith Inch."

In May, 1882, it was announced that the contingents from Peterhead, Banff, Cullen, Fraserburgh, Gardenstown, Macduff, and Portsoy were to be amalgamated as the 1st Buchan Artillery Volunteers.

The Corps of Rifle Volunteers at Peterhead

Riflemen were more hesitant in "coming forward" than artillerymen had been. By mid-January, 1860, however, about 100 had expressed an interest in joining and the Feuars had given £20 towards the cost of forming a Corps. A month later, Captain Anderson of the 78th Highlanders had, after inspection, authorised a range suitable for practice; Sergeant Simpson of the 92nd Highlanders had taken up his post as Instructor; and a local businessman, Adam Gray, had offered the use of a hall for exercise during bad weather. Eventually, on 7th March, 1860, the War Office formally sanctioned a Corps of Rifle Volunteers at Peterhead, which was numbered the 21st in the County of Aberdeen. Its establishment was Captain Commandant, Captain, 2 Lieutenants, 2 Ensigns, Assistant Surgeon, and 200 men of all ranks, divided into two companies. "Slowly but

surely does Red Tape perform its functions," commented the *Sentinel*. "After a delay which was awakening the anxiety of our Riflemen, even although they were being kept "oot o' langer" by the drill, their services have been accepted. A communication to that effect has just been received from the War Office and last night it was read to a portion of the corps met for exercise in Broad Place Pavilion. They were formed into a square for the purpose and scarcely had the secretary finished his pleasing task when the hall re-echoed with the most enthusiastic cheering. A special and truly loyal salute was given for the Queen."

By the beginning of April, 1860, the War Office had confirmed the appointment of the locally elected officers. The Captain Commandant was William Alexander of Springhill; T. J. Bremner was Captain; C. Noble of Berryhill and T. Arbuthnot Jr. were respectively First and Second Lieutenant; the Ensigns were Alex. Walker of Richmond and John Mackintosh, Gas Manager; and Dr. Anderson became Assistant Surgeon.

Each effective member had to provide his own uniform and was responsible for the preservation of all articles issued to him. The penalty for loading contrary to orders or shooting out of turn was 2s.6d (12½p). Anybody who discharged a rifle accidentally or pointed a rifle, loaded or unloaded, at any person without orders, was fined 5s (25p). Talking in the ranks, while at attention, incurred a fine of 6d (2½p), and anyone absent from a prescribed drill had to pay 2d (less than 1p)!

There were 145 enrolments by the second week in May, 1860, but no uniforms nor rifles had been issued when, at the end of the month, the programme for the summer was announced. Drill was scheduled at 6.30 a.m. and 8.00 p.m. on Tuesdays and Fridays, when the roll was called, and at 4.00 p.m. on Saturdays. Significantly, volunteers did not have to ask for time off work but could be on parade before or after working hours and so would not lose wages. That the longer working hours prevalent in Victorian times had an inhibiting effect on recruitment is implicit in the comment in the *Sentinel*, "During the summer months, solicitors in the town are to allow clerks and apprentices to leave their offices at 7 instead of 8 in the evening - by which no small boon has been conferred - from 15th April to 15th September."

Morale remained high in spite of the lack of uniforms and rifles. A drum, part of the paraphernalia of the local militia during the Napoleonic Wars, was re-conditioned for the use of the Corps; non-commissioned officers - four sergeants and four corporals - were elected; and arrangements were made for the formation of a Rifle Corps Band.On

17th August, 1860, the *Sentinel* carried the following advertisement : "Wanted for Peterhead Rifle Corps a person acquainted with the use and cleaning of MUSKETS to become storekeeper". By this time, one of the lower apartments of the Town House had been fitted up as an armoury; the Band was fully equipped; and the corps had turned out on several occasions in full uniform, with rifles and bayonets. Tunic, trousers, and cap - medium grey with red and black facings - were supplied by an Aberdeen outfitter for £1.17s (£1.85) while the lowest tender for supplying the belts had been submitted by a local saddler.

Emphasising that "A large amount of Funds will be required to maintain the efficiency of the Corps, and especially to fit out those who cannot afford their own Uniform and Equipment", the Corps Committee decided, as "a means of supplementing Subscriptions", to hold a Grand Military Bazaar, on 7th September, "under the distinguished patronage of the Countess of Erroll and a Committee of Management of the Ladies of Peterhead and district". A special request was made to employers to allow members of the Corps to assemble at 10.30 a.m. prior to marching to the bazaar where, with the Band playing "appropriate airs", they paraded in front of the hall. After a general salute as the Band played *God Save The Queen*, spectators joined the Volunteers in giving three cheers for Her Majesty and the Corps returned to the Armoury to deposit their arms and be dismissed.

Although the Grand Military Bazaar made £150, new recruits to the Rifle Corps were still expected to contribute towards the cost of their outfit. The next advertisement inviting enrolments warned potential recruits that "None need apply unless prepared to pay by instalments, or otherwise, at least to the extent of £1 towards the expense of the uniform."

The Corps of Rifle Volunteers at Peterhead was designated the 9th Aberdeenshire Rifle Corps on 7th December, 1860. Two weeks later, the Corps held a Ball for which each member was given a ticket for a lady. The *Sentinel* reported that music was provided by an "orchestra of violins, violincello, clarionet (sic), harmonium, etc." and that the company went through to supper, "by numbers", under the supervision of Sgt. Simpson. When a similar function was organised in January, 1862, the *Sentinel* intimated tersely, "We believe a Rifle Volunteer Ball took place on Friday evening, last. Not having been furnished with the usual press courtesy ticket, we can give no report whatever of the proceedings."

The editor's pique was short-lived and did not prevent his reporting the newsworthy activities of the Corps. On 8th May, 1863, for example, readers were informed that "The Rifle Band gave a performance of

upward of half an hour on the Tolbooth Green. Several fine airs were performed in fine style, thus evincing the degree of efficiency to which they have of late attained. The crowd, however, pressed in on the performers so much as to seriously discommode them and a number of urchins seemed quite determined to drown the music with their noise. We would suggest to the police to keep a little order on these occasions. If the Band put themselves to the trouble of favouring the public with their performances, they ought to be allowed to do so to the utmost advantage."

A *Competition for Gold and Silver Medals*, was organised in September and October, 1862. After each competitor had fired five rounds at 300 yards (about 274 metres), standing, and five rounds at 400 yards (about 365 metres), standing, the six best shots were selected to represent the local Corps during in the forthcoming Battalion competition. This, the 3rd Aberdeenshire (or Buchan) Administrative Battalion of the Rifle Volunteers, with its headquarters in Peterhead, consisted of the 5th or New Deer Corps, the 9th or Peterhead Corps, the 17th or Old Deer Corps, and the 20th or Longside Corps.

In the week following the local rifle competition, another Grand Military Bazaar was held in the Pavilion, Broad Place, on 9th and 10th October. "Admission dues" were sixpence (2½p) on the first day and threepence on the second day; a Family Ticket, giving admission on both days for three or more, cost one shilling and sixpence (7½p). Non-Commissioned Officers and Privates of the Volunteer Services, in uniform, were admitted for threepence. Mrs. Dingwall Fordyce of Brucklay (*K4* on page 116) was responsible for the New Deer Table; Mrs. Captain Alexander and Mrs. Captain Bremner for the Peterhead Table; Mrs. Russell of Aden (*K5* on page 116) for the Old Deer Table; and Mrs. Hutchison of Cairngall for the Longside Table. In addition, there was a "Refreshment Table to which contributions of Fruit, Cheese Cakes, Custards, Tarts, Jellies, Sandwiches, Ginger Beer, Lemonade, and other articles usually provided on such occasions will be thankfully received."

The *Sentinel* drew attention to a folding fire screen which had been especially made for the occasion and was the prize in a lottery. It also highlighted some of the outstanding items for sale - a vase of polished Peterhead granite, which was bought for the Merchant Maiden Hospital, Edinburgh; a fender stool; an ottoman; cushions; a crochet bed cover; tapestry and worsted work; specimens of native beadwork sent from New Brunswick by the Honourable Arthur Gordon, Lieutenant-Governor; specimens of "Parisian and Italian fancy work presented by Mrs. Russell of Aden" and, on the New

Deer Table, which had the "largest supply of articles with a fair market value of upwards of £100", the item most likely to attract attention was "a beautiful piece of silk Japanese work representing three herons rising from a marsh."

The *Sentinel* also recommended "a little publication bearing the title of *Military Bazaar Gazette*, which was "full of good-natured local jokes, with neatly got-up little articles suited especially for the occasion, and besides contains a very good wood-cut portrait of

K4 Brucklay Castle, home of the Dingwall and later the Dingwall-Fordyce families was re-constructed in 1765, 1814, and 1849 to create "a mansion of the old Scottish castellated style."

K5 Aden House - home of the Russell family from 1758 until 1937 - as it was after re-consruction by John Smith, Aberdeen City Architect, in 1832.

Mr. Gammack, who has done so much for the cause of Volunteering in Buchan." W. L. Taylor included this "Gazette" in his *Bibliography of Peterhead Literature* with the information that the wood-cut was from a photograph by Joseph Collier and that the publication, which cost twopence, was "Registered for transmission to Longside, Old Deer, Boddam, and the Cannibal Islands"!

The Corps continued to follow its scheduled routine of drills, exercises, and inspections. Regular participation in these activities became vitally important after the Volunteer Act, 1863, outlined the criteria for the annual issue, on 1st December, of Certificates of Efficiency. Rifle Corps recruits were not eligible for assessment until they had served a probationary period of eighteen months during which they had to attend instruction in musketry and Squad, Company, or Battalion Drills on at least thirty occasions. Before qualifying for a Certificate of Efficiency, which remained valid for one year, the "old hands" were required to attend at least six Battalion and three Company Drills per year and, since Inspecting Officers were empowered to identify individuals who were not proficient, to have been present at the last inspection.

The four Corps of Rifle Volunteers in Buchan - the 5th at New Deer, the 9th at Peterhead, the 17th at Old Deer, and the 20th at Longside - had been united as the 3rd Administrative Aberdeenshire Battalion in January, 1862. Two years later, it was known as the 3rd (or Buchan) Administrative Battalion. The Battalion was kept at an acceptable level of efficiency by regular reviews, inspections, and "sham fights". Many of the officers gained Certificates of Proficiency after attending courses at training depots as far afield as the Tower of London, Aldershot, Manchester, St. George's Barracks, Wellington Barracks, and Chelsea Barracks.

In 1871, now armed with the Snider rifle, the Battalion was one of the first in Scotland to go under canvas. Commanded by Lieutenant Colonel Russell, the Riflemen pitched camp near the South Lodge at Aden, in a field sloping down to the South Ugie. The innovation was a success and two years later, the Battalion camped again at Aden. In subsequent years, successful camps were held on estates owned by the current Commanding Officer: at Pitfour under Lieutenant Colonel John Ferguson and at Shevado, near Brucklay Castle, under Lieutenant Colonel Fordyce.

The proceeds from a Bazaar in the Music Hall went towards the estimated cost of £1500 for a Drill Hall which was built near the southern end of the town in 1880. It accommodated a Committee Room, an Orderly Room, and the Sergeant-Instructor's House, as well as a hall for drilling the Volunteers.

When the first four Corps of Rifle Volunteers in Buchan were amalgamated as the 3rd Administrative Aberdeenshire Battalion, each Corps retained its own uniform - dark grey with red facings at New Deer; medium grey with red and black facings at Peterhead; Elcho grey with blue piping and black braid at Old Deer; and dark grey with black facings at Longside. In August, 1863, however, it was decided to adopt Government Grey cloth with black facings for the Battalion uniform of tunic, trousers, and gaiters. In 1868, rifle green cloth with red piping was used and, four years later, the chaco (shako) was replaced by a new pattern of rifle busby. In May, 1880, the component Corps of the 3rd Administrative Aberdeenshire Battalion and the Rifle Corps at St. Fergus, New Pitsligo, Cruden, and Fraserburgh were consolidated as the 3rd Aberdeenshire (The Buchan) Rifle Volunteer Corps. The busby was replaced by "an invisible green Glengarry with scarlet dicing as a full head-dress" with a badge of a St. Andrews Cross in a scroll bordered with thistles and bearing the designation of the Battalion. Three years later, this Battalion adopted Gordon tartan trews and the Glengarry diced forage cap of the Gordon Highlander pattern.

The Corps was re-named The 3rd (The Buchan) Volunteer Battalion of the Gordon Highlanders in January, 1884. The locally focused component Companies were A - New Deer; B- Peterhead; C - Crimond, Lonmay, and St. Fergus; D - Old Deer; E - Strichen; F - Longside; G - Fraserburgh; H - Fraserburgh and New Pitsligo; I - Cruden; and K - Peterhead and Boddam. The new Battalion's uniform consisted of a scarlet Highland doublet with yellow facings, tartan trews of the Gordon tartan (green with a single yellow stripe), and diced (white, red, and green) Glengarry cap. The cap badge had a stag's head rising from a coronet upon a wreath of ivy and the motto *By Dand*. The regimental march was the air of the well-known local song *O! Logie o' Buchan. O! Logie the Laird*.

In 1885, with a total enrolled strength of 919, the Battalion was armed with the Martini-Henry rifle; in 1888, a signalling class was begun and the Battalion became part of the Highland Brigade, one of the first Volunteer Brigades to be established. In 1892, when the Earl of Erroll was appointed Honorary Colonel of the Battalion, a cyclist section was formed and sixteen Volunteers, who had gained Army Ambulance Certificates, became regimental stretcher-bearers.

The 3rd Volunteer Battalion was obviously preparing to play its part in any action involving the Highland Brigade. It was also available to make an appropriate contribution on ceremonial occasions. On 26th

K6 *Officers of the Buchan Rifle Volunteers, 1875.*

K7 *The Band of the 9th Aberdeenshire Rifle Volunteers; David Alexander, Bandmaster. December, 1875.*

January, 1901, for example, four days after Queen Victoria died, the *Sentinel* announced that "Members of the 3rd Volunteer Gordon Highlanders will parade at the Drill Hall To-Day, at 1.45 p.m., to form a Guard of Honour at the Proclamation of King Edward VII. Dress - Full Uniform." The Volunteers duly paraded, at 2.30 p.m., "at the Cross, Broad Street," i.e. the Reform Monument, where sixteen of them joined sixteen Naval Reservists, and sixteen Artillery Volunteers to form a Guard of Honour. Instructions for the Proclamation to be made on 26th January had been received the previous day and this short notice may account for the lukewarm report in the *Buchan Observer* : "The ceremony lasted a few minutes only and could not be called impressive, but it was interesting in some ways and notwithstanding that the weather was snowy and bitterly cold, it attracted an enormous crowd of spectators." All the public bodies in the town, including *Free Masons, Master Builders Association, Peterhead Oddfellows Friendly Society, Erroll Lodge of Free Gardeners, Marshal Keith Lodge of Oddfellows, Independent Order of Rechabites, Loyal Order of Ancient Shepherds,* and *Peterhead Fishermen's Benevolent Society,* were represented. The police were helped in their efforts to marshal the crowd by contingents from the Naval Reserve the Artillery Volunteers, and the 3rd Volunteer Battalion Gordon Highlanders, who were deployed at both sides of the street and also formed a corridor through which the official party could walk in procession from the Town House to the platform, which had been erected near the Reform Munument. The Proclamation of the new monarch, King Edward VII, officially ended the Victorian era.